The Revelation of Jesus Christ as Told to His Servant John

A VERSE-BY-VERSE STUDY

Carleton Fletcher Burrows, Jr.

TRILOGY CHRISTIAN PUBLISHERS

Tustin, CA

Trilogy Christian Publishers
A Wholly Owned Subsidary of Trinity Broadcasting Network
2442 Michelle Drive
Tustin, CA 92780

The Revelation of Jesus Christ as Told to His Servant John

Cover artwork by Caran Burrows Leahy

For information about special discounts for bulk purchases, please contact Trilogy Christian Publishing.

Manufactured in the United States of America

10 9 8 7 6 5 4 3 2 1

Library of Congress Cataloging-in-Publication Data is available.

ISBN: 978-1-68556-274-8

E-ISBN: 978-1-68556-275-5 (ebook)

Contents

Introduction

In 1909, C. I. Scofield wrote in his notes on the book of Revelation: "That which is designedly obscure to us will be clear to those for whom it was written as the time approaches."

Today, we are approximately one hundred years down the line in time, and we can see that the book of Revelation has indeed become much clearer. As a matter of fact, not only is this book easier to understand, it appears that we are living in the time of the countdown to the events within this book.

There are those who believe that the book of Revelation is a closed book and one which we are not intended to understand. I believe it is open to all who are willing to do the work required to understand it.

It cannot be denied that this book confused many people, including some great spiritual men, but in the same breath, that has been of immeasurable blessing, for it reveals God's plan for the future. On days such as these we live in today, world conditions are uncertain, and many people are asking, "What does the future hold for me?"

The book of Revelation reveals what the future holds. The revelation is given to God's people, and as the events recorded in this book unfold, the student of Scripture need not be taken by surprise. It is possible, through studying this book, to know God's plan for the future.

While many have a hard time comprehending what the book of Revelation is talking about, we must remember that the apostle John wrote down what was presented to him. His writings were circulated throughout the seven churches of Asia Minor, where they were read and understood. Therefore, if they could understand these writings 2,000 years ago, then so can we today!

As we begin to look at this book, we must understand that it contains many things and events that are still featured to us. If we have trouble understanding events still future to us, imagine the huge problem John had when he was confronted with things from our present, such as planes, trains, and automobiles. And he wrote of things that are still to come in our future.

As we begin, these are your guidelines to follow for proper interpretation: Firstly, the Bible is true and accurate. Secondly, if we follow all the rules of biblical interpretation, in this study, we will get a complete understanding of what God has in store for us.

Before we get into the text, I would like to set some simple, special rules for interpreting the book of Revelation. Keep in mind that most of the text of this book still refers to the future. If it was difficult for John to explain what he had seen, we will also encounter things that are difficult for us to understand and explain. So, as we begin, we must follow the golden rule of interpretation whenever possible. That is, when the plain sense of a scripture makes common sense, seek no other sense, lest it become nonsense.

This means that we must take every word at its prime—its primary, ordinary, usual literal meaning—unless effects of the immediate text, when two related passages are compared, and fundamental truths of the Bible indicate otherwise. These rules will provide helpful and basic guidelines for interpreting the many signs and symbols that we will encounter.

The book of Revelation is not written chronologically. We may see a specific event written down and elaborated on several chapters later, and we need to make sure that we keep in mind where the activity is located. There are sudden shifts in scenes. One chapter will be speaking about an event on the earth and suddenly seen shifting to one in heaven. Time is also a factor since some events will take place in the first three and a half years of the Tribulation and others in the last three and a half years.

There will be many questions that will arise and be addressed as we move through Scripture. I will try to anticipate these questions so the answers will be in context with the Scripture texts.

But information is not available to ensure that there is a way that some questions can be answered. So, I use the following guidance. When I began to study the Bible, I had a wise professor who told me to keep *a rainy-day book of questions*. "Some," he told me, "will be answered in time; others will have to wait till we go to be with the Lord."

One last thing: I do not claim to be the last word on this book. I have read many books written on the book of Revelation, and they were written by those who also studied and dedicated much time to the book. I ask that you consider what I have gathered from my study; this study is the first verse-by-verse study of the message given to the apostle John by our Lord and Savior Jesus Christ, and as far as I know, the only study that attempts to include every verse in the account. May God give His approval for this effort and make you, the reader, people blessed by the content.

Chapter One

"The Revelation of Jesus Christ, which God gave him to show unto his servants, even the things which must shortly come to pass: and he sent and signified by his angel unto his servant John" (verse one; hereinafter, unless otherwise indicated, the verses are from Revelation; chapters of the book match chapters in Revelation).

The word "revelation" comes from the Greek word *apokalypsis*, which means "an unveiling." It means "to show" or "expose to view." This, then, is the unveiling of a message from Jesus Christ. It is a message that God the Father gave Him: (1) to show to His people, or the church, things that must *shortly* come to pass; and (2) He sent it and signified His message by His *angelos*, or messenger. To "signify" is to authenticate the message and *the messenger*. The message was given to John, a slave (not servant) of Jesus Christ (Greek: doulos).

"Who bare witness of the word of God, and of the testimony of Jesus Christ, even of all things he saw" (verse two).

The last book of the New Testament was written by the apostle John who was an eye witness to the ministry, life, death, resurrection, and ascension of Jesus Christ, whom John identifies in the Gospel according to John as the *Incarnate Word of God*

(God in the flesh of man) or Jesus, who called John to be His apostle, and John, as an elderly man, gives his personal testimony to all of the events to which he was privy concerning Jesus Christ and everything he saw Him do in his presence.

"Blessed is he that readeth, and they that hear the words of the prophecy, and keep the things that are written therein: for the time is at hand" (verse three).

We see in this verse that a blessing is offered to those who read, hear, and keep the *words of this book*. A "blessing" as used in Scripture means *to be happy*. As we know, happiness, in the spiritual sense, is not found in things of this world but from God. Therefore, the happiness, or blessedness, spoken of here has its source in the words of this book of prophecy. If we read it and let it sink into our minds, hear it in the depths of our hearts, and obey its instructions, we will be happy because we know we are living in the will of God.

"The time is at hand" means simply that from the time of the writing of this book until all of the events come to be a reality, nothing else on God's timetable needs to happen before the prophecy in this book begins to happen.

It is possible that we are living in the time when these things begin to unfold. We know, from studying the Bible, that it could be tomorrow or that it could be another 1,000 years until this prophecy is fulfilled.

"John to the seven churches that are in Asia: Grace to you and peace, from him who is and was and who is to come; and from the seven spirits that are before his throne" (verse four).

We see that John is the scribe who is penning this epistle and that he is addressing it to the seven churches that had been established in Asia Minor (which is modern-day Turkey). He begins by extending God's *grace and peace*. Grace is the divine love and protection that God bestows on those who belong to Him. *Peace* is that inner contentment, or freedom from strife, which a Christian has in his or her position of salvation through Jesus Christ. This allows him or her complete assurance of eternal life. One's relationship with God determines whether one will have this *grace and peace*. In this verse, we see a reference to the eternal God: "From him who is and who was and who is to come." Whenever we see the word "God" in Scripture, we should look at it carefully to determine whether it is referring to *God the Father, God the Son, God the Holy Spirit, or the collective Trinity.*

In this case, it refers to the collective triune God since this expression connotes the eternality of God. It is significant to note that this book has its origin in the Trinity. We see the triune nature again in verse eight of this chapter.

The "seven spirits" is a reference to the sevenfold work of the Holy Spirit, which is shown in Isaiah 11:2 where He is referred to as the Spirit of God, the Spirit of wisdom, the Spirit of understanding, the Spirit of counsel, the Spirit of might, the Spirit of knowledge, and the Spirit of the fear of God. Thus, the term *seven spirits* does not refer to seven different Holy Spirits but to the seven ministries of one Holy Spirit.

"And from Jesus Christ, who is the faithful witness, the firstborn of the dead, and the ruler of the kings of the earth. Unto him that loveth us, and loosed us from our sins by his blood" (verse five).

All that men need to know about God has been revealed to them by Jesus Christ. He told Philip, "He who has seen Me has

3

seen the Father" (John 14:9, NKJV). His witness is sufficient. He is identified as the firstborn of the dead, being the first one ever to be resurrected. There were others who were raised from the dead, but they all died natural deaths later.

They were not raised in incorruption. Jesus is the only one ever to be raised in His glorified incorruptible body.

Although it now seems as though others rule, Jesus is the One who will, one day, rule over the earth from His throne in Jerusalem, and He will be *the King of kings and the Lord of lords to the glory of the Father* (Revelation 19:16).

It is this Jesus who has done away with our sins through His death on the cross. We are cleansed from our sinful natures only because of His sacrifice for us.

"And he made us to be a kingdom, to be priests unto his God and Father; to him be the glory and the dominion for ever and ever. Amen" (verse six).

Amazing as it may seem, Jesus has made us, the church, a royal kingdom. We are the citizens of the eternal kingdom of God! We are the kingdom. He has also made us priests in the holy kingdom. In 1 Peter 2:9, the church is said to be "an elect race, a royal priesthood," and again, here in the book of Revelation 5:10, we are told *we will reign with Jesus when He sits on the throne in Jerusalem.*

Right now, not too many Christians even consider their future. Many cannot even comprehend that we will literally be the priests of God. While we may not act like priests, look like priests, think like priests, or imagine that we could ever be priests, the Scriptures say it is so. The Scriptures have no errors, and all of the credit and honor will go to God, for He made it to be so.

"Behold, he cometh with the clouds; and every eye shall see him, and they that pierced him; and all of the tribes of the earth shall mourn over him. Even so, Amen" (verse seven).

Jesus is coming again! This is chiseled in granite! This is a certified, guaranteed promise that can never be revoked. In Acts 1:11, it tells us, "This Jesus, who was received up from you into heaven shall so come in like manner as ye beheld him going into heaven."

When He comes, it will be a physical, visible appearance. At the end of the Tribulation period, Jesus will come to set up His kingdom. When He comes, He will come in the clouds. He will be coming in power and glory, and every eye will see Him. This doesn't mean just those people who are alive on the earth at the time. It means every eye...all people, from the creation to Jesus' coming, will see Him as He descends from heaven to set up His kingdom and take the throne of David to reign forever!

The mention of those who pierced Him refers to the disbelieving Jews who rejected Him when He came as Savior, including the chief priests, Caiaphas and Annas, who are among the actual people who rejected Jesus. But from the New Testament point of view, these people were acting as representatives for all mankind of all time, for it also refers to those who have rejected Him since. These have done what the Bible says in Hebrews 6:6: "They crucify to themselves the Son of God afresh."

"I am the Alpha and the Omega, saith the Lord God, who is and who was and who is to come, the Almighty" (verse eight).

Such a stupendous statement needs more than the Prophet's own signature or even Jesus Christ's "amen." God the Father Himself speaks and, with His signature, vouches for the truthfulness of the coming Jesus Christ.

There are three strong names of God in this verse: Alpha and Omega, the Lord God who is and was and is to come, and the Almighty.

Alpha and *omega* are the first and last letters in the Greek alphabet, or the beginning and the end. Only the book of Revelation refers to God the Father as *Alpha and Omega*. He is the source of all creation of history, and He is the end of all things. Nothing exists outside of His creation.

Therefore, He is the Lord God! He has always existed, so He was. He still exists, so He is, and He will always exist. He is the Creator and Sustainer, and in order to be all of these, He has to be the almighty God.

With verse eight, the salutation from God is concluded. The primary reason for the salutation is to provide testimony to the person and program of Jesus Christ. Jesus Christ is the central character of this book. All things begin and end with Him. He controls the conflicts and catastrophic judgments that fill the major portion of this book. He is the soon-to-come King who will defeat His enemies and reclaim planet Earth. He is the One who will create a new heaven and a new earth, in which He will place the new Jerusalem to house the righteous citizens for eternity.

> I John, your brother and partaker with you in tribu-
> lation and kingdom and patience which are in Jesus
> Christ, was in the isle that is called Patmos, for the
> word of God and the testimony of Jesus.
>
> Verse nine

The apostle John begins this verse by identifying himself for his readers and describing the setting where he received the message about which he is writing. He describes himself as a fellow believer with those who are in the kingdom of God. (Actually, the kingdom is still future, but all who believe in Christ will be a part of the spiritual kingdom.)

John had been banished to the isle of Patmos as a religious and political prisoner by Emperor Domitian in AD 95. John was exiled for faithfully preaching and teaching the Word of God and for the testimony he gave for Jesus Christ.

Patmos is a small, isolated, mostly volcanic island, only ten miles long and six miles wide, located in the Aegean Sea. The aged apostle was made to do hard labor in the mines on Patmos. He was released by Emperor Nerva eighteen months later.

John was sustained during this time by the *patience* of Jesus Christ. That is, Christ provided the needed strength for him to endure his trial and come through it victoriously.

"I was in the Spirit on the Lord's day, and I heard behind me a great voice, as of a trumpet" (verse ten).

John received a vision on a Sunday. This is the first of four visions John received *while in the Spirit* (Revelation 1:10, 4:2, 17:3, and 21:10). Being *in the Spirit* is being under the control of the Holy Spirit, and under His control, John received a mental, visual picture of the events given.

In this state, John heard a voice behind him that was loud and clear,

> saying, What thou seest, write in a book and send it to the seven churches: unto Ephesus, and unto Smyrna, and unto Pergamum, and unto Thyatira, and unto Sardis, and unto Philadelphia, and unto Laodicea.
>
> Verse eleven

The apostle was commanded to write down what was shown to him and send it to the seven churches that are in Asia. This is the first of twelve times that John was commanded to write down what he saw.

The Revelation of Jesus Christ was then penned by John in the eighteen months he was a prisoner on Patmos and then passed on to the churches of Asia Minor as instructed.

The recipients of the letter were the seven churches that have been established in Asia Minor, which we know of as modern-day Turkey. Each city is depicted as a type of person:

Ephesus, shifty, changing, and undependable; Smyrna, fortunate in many ways but always suffering; Pergamum, in possession of power but corrupted by others who were attracted to the power; Thyatira, basically good but without moral strength to stand up for its convictions; Sardis, complacent and satisfied, willfully unaware that principles and morals were dying; Philadelphia, weak but with hidden sources of stamina; Laodicea, sophisticated, wealthy, shrewd but spiritually empty.

"And I turned to see the voice that spake with me. And having turned I saw seven golden candlesticks" (verse twelve).

When John heard the voice behind him, he turned to see who was speaking. The first thing he saw was a group of seven golden candlesticks. There is no description of these candlesticks, only that they were golden, and the number of them was seven.

"And in the midst of the candlesticks one like unto a son of man, clothed with a garment down to the foot, and girt about the breasts with a golden girdle" (verse thirteen).

There is no indication of how the candlesticks were arranged, but this verse tells us that someone was standing among them. John identifies him as someone resembling the Son of Man, or Jesus. The word "like" indicates that there was something about this man that John remembered, but He was still familiar. We know now that this was the glorified Jesus. He still had His human form, but His appearance had changed. His dress was that of someone of royal position. He was wearing a girdle of gold wound around a garment that came down to the feet. This was in contrast to the normal dress of an Israeli, which is a short robe held in place by a rope or sash. The material for an ordinary robe was generally gray or brown in color but never white.

"And his head and his hair were white as white wool, white as snow; and his eyes were as a flame of fire" (verse fourteen).

The last time John had seen Jesus, He had the dark hair of a thirty-three-year-old man. Now His hair was white. John's description is the same as seen in Daniel 7:9. White hair in Scripture is symbolic of purity in character, wisdom, dignity of age, authority as a judge, and eternality. The brightness here could have been from the brightness of Jesus' glory.

His eyes had a penetrating gaze that flashed and had the look of divine wrath upon the wicked. "Eyes like fire" is a biblical statement of judgment.

"And his feet like unto burnished brass, as if it had been refined in a furnace; and his voice as the voice of many waters" (verse fifteen).

Burnished brass is pure polished brass, refined in the fire, and extraordinarily strong. This is symbolic of Christ's strength as He treads the wicked in judgment, ultimately making His enemies His footstool (Hebrews 10:13).

The *voice of many waters* is like the sound of a great waterfall. If you have ever been to Niagara Falls and have heard the roar of the falls, you will have an idea of the sound. It is so loud you can hear nothing else.

"And he had in his right hand seven stars: and out of his mouth proceeded a sharp two-edged sword: and his countenance was as the sun shineth in his strength" (verse sixteen).

Jesus had seven stars in His right hand. We will see a description of these stars in verse twenty. Holding something in the right hand indicates safety and power. Stars are associated with angels in both the Old Testament (Job 38:7) and the New

Testament (Revelation 9:1) as faithful witnesses to God (Daniel 12:3).

John identifies Jesus as having a sharp two-edged sword coming out of His mouth. This was the type of sword used by the Greeks. The two edges of the sword are indicative of His Word. In Hebrews 4:12, we read:

> For the word of God is living, and active, and sharper than any two-edged sword, and piercing even to the dividing of the soul and spirit, of both joints and marrow, and quick to discern the thoughts and intents of the heart.

This metaphor is important for three reasons: John refers to this characteristic of Jesus several times, in Revelation 1:16; 2:12, 16; 19:15, 21. He uses a rare word for sword (Greek: *rhomphaia*), which is used only one time outside of the book of Revelation in Luke 2:35, and there is no spiritual parallel to the expression except in Isaiah 11:14, where it prophesies that the Messiah *will strike the earth with the sword of His mouth.*

The short sword was used for close-quarters combat and allowed a soldier to cut quickly, coming and going, and the judgment of Jesus will be quick and entire. He looks deep into the hearts of men and is able to discern the entire man totally.

Finally, the face of Jesus is compared to the sun, shining in all its brilliance. This is an indication that Jesus was showing His divine glory. This glory has a radiance that is much brighter than the sun. The Old Testament says *no man has looked upon the glory of God and lived* (Exodus 33:20). His brightness is such that just to look at Him in our present human form is to die at the sight of Him. It is only because He is approaching man in judgment that they will not burn up immediately. He has His final message to deliver to them before they go into eternity.

"And when I saw him, I fell at his feet as one dead. And he laid his right hand upon me, saying, Fear not; I am the first and the last" (verse seventeen).

This is the same time as when John laid his head on Jesus' breast in the Upper Room. He now faints and falls down at Jesus' feet, knocked out by the glory of the resurrected and glorified Jesus Christ.

As Jesus laid His hand on John, He told him, "Fear not." Jesus often used the term *fear not*, and He gives John a reason: He is the *Alpha and Omega*, the *First and the Last*. He speaks of His eternality. He existed before there was anything, and He will still exist after all things are finished. The beginning and the end!

"And the Living one; and I was dead, and behold, I am alive for evermore, and I have the keys of death and Hades" (verse eighteen).

The Scriptures tell us that Jesus died to sin, *once for all* (Romans 6:10), and that *He will live forevermore* (Revelation 10:6). He will not change His state of glory again, and He will always be.

Jesus then shares a detail that John didn't reveal before: Jesus has in His hands some keys. He has purchased these keys with His own blood. Hebrews 2:14–15 says that in the final judgment, Jesus will use these keys to close the gates of hell forever, and in eternity there will be no more death. The Christian need not fear death because "through death he might bring to nought him that had the power of death, that is, the devil" (Hebrews 2:14), "and might deliver all them who through fear of death were all their lifetime subject to bondage" (Hebrews 2:15). These keys are the symbol of eternal release for Christians, but men without Christ have every reason to fear, for they will face the second death for eternity. We will see another reference to these keys later in the letter to the church in Philadelphia.

"Write therefore the things which thou sawest, and the things which are, and the things which shall come to pass in the hereafter" (verse nineteen).

John was instructed to begin writing. He was to write down everything he had personally seen. He was to cover the past, what was happening in the present, and those things that Jesus showed him that would happen in the future.

> The mystery of the seven stars which thou sawest in my right hand, and the seven golden candlesticks. The seven stars are the angels of the seven churches: and the seven candlesticks are seven churches.
>
> Verse twenty

And now we find out about those *seven stars*, which Jesus had in His right hand, and the *seven golden candlesticks*: Jesus solves the mystery for us! The "seven stars" are the *angels of the seven churches of Asia Minor*. In the Greek language, an angel is a messenger from God. These messengers could have been heavenly beings, or they could have been the pastors of the churches, for both were given messages from God to share with His people.

The difference is this: at the inception of the church, God spoke directly to certain men. These men wrote down what they were told and passed the information around to the entire church throughout the known world. As we will see at the end of this study, when John completed the penning of the book of Revelation, it was the end of direct messages from God. Today, God's messengers get their information and inspiration from the printed Word. Yet, even now, God still speaks to us through His Holy Spirit.

The *seven golden candlesticks are the seven churches of Asia Minor.* Take note: in many cases in the book of Revelation, symbols, such as the golden candlesticks, are explained in the text. When we get to chapter seventeen, I will show you a very interesting interpretation error that has been taught for the last fifty years, when the correct interpretation is written down for us to see plainly.

But for now, the seven candlesticks are the seven churches of Asia!

Chapter Two

The Church in Ephesus

The name *Ephesus* means "desired" or "desirable," a term applied by a lover to a woman of his choice. The name is also defined as "shifty," after the nature of the city's location, which was swampy, and because of the constant shifting of the channels of its harbor, caused by silting of the River Cayster. The city of Ephesus was founded in 1087 BC. Androklos, son of the legendary Athenian King Codrus, was the founder. He consulted an oracle, or crystal-ball gazer, at Delphi and was told that a fish would show him the place for a new colony and that a boar would lead them to the future site of the city, which would be named Ephesus. While they were preparing a fish dinner on the shore of the Aegean, the fish jumped out of the pan. Startled, the cook dropped the pan, which started a brush fire, which, in turn, startled a boar. Androklos followed the boar and eventually killed it. The spot on which he killed the boar became the site where he built the city. There was a small settlement, which was the first Ephesus, and to make way for his city, Androklos razed the original.

The fact that there was a good spot for a harbor, fertile land nearby, and a freshwater stream flowing into the river, was, of course, helpful. Ephesus had one of the best-protected harbors in Asia Minor on the Aegean Sea. The gulf of Ephesus, or the Caystrian Gulf, was formed on the north by a projection of the coast, ending in the Argennum promontory and the island of Chios, and on the south by Mount Mycele, ending on the Trogyllium promontory (see Acts 20:15) and the island of Samos. These natural advantages assured Ephesus the attention of ships carrying commercial goods throughout the entire Aegean area. A long mountain ridge runs east of Ephesus and divides the valley of the Cayster River from the valley of the Meander River. Ephesus had easy access to both valleys, by which the traveler or merchant could reach the inland regions of Asia Minor. The fame and success of Ephesus were practically assured by its location on the protected gulf and on the natural overland route of the southern arm of the great trade route from the Orient.

The city itself was located on an alluvial plain of the Cayster River, a stream that descends from the southern slopes of Mount Tmolus. The Cayster terminated at the harbor of Ephesus, and the amount of silt that it deposited was a constant problem. Historically speaking, the Ephesians were aware of the harbor's importance for the prosperity of the city, but despite constant dredging, it silted up. All their efforts were in vain, and the Aegean seacoast is now five miles away from the ruins of the city. The silting had come, primarily, from the Romans systematically stripping the hillsides of trees for wood, which they made into charcoal.

Ephesus became the most important Greek city in Asia Minor. After the colony was started, one of the first religions to be practiced was the worship of the mother goddess, Cybele, as was common throughout Asia Minor. The Greek name for Cybele was Artemis, and a small temple was built, which would later become the great Temple of Artemis.

In 133 BC, Alexander liberated all of the Ionian cities from the Seleucids, traveled to Ephesus, and paid special attention to the Temple of Artemis. It had burned down and was being rebuilt in even greater splendor than it had originally. Alexander supported the reconstruction. Thus, Ephesus became not only a great trade center but also a city of pilgrimage of those who worshiped Artemis.

In 294 BC, Lysimachus, one of Alexander's generals, rebuilt and enlarged Ephesus but shifted the site to a new location away from the swampy river edge. He moved it to its third site, in the valley between Mount Pion and the Koressos ridge. This is the site we know from Scripture. The inhabitants were reluctant to move to the new site. To encourage the move, Lysimachus filled the sewage pipes with cement so that the sewage system could not be used. As can be imagined, the city was abandoned, and in a short time, the new Ephesus became the most densely populated city of its time, having a population of upward of 500,000 citizens.

The Seleucid regime, which inherited this area's part of Alexander's empire, continually renewed this city's privileges. Since the Seleucids were Greek, Ephesus prospered enormously as terminals for caravans traveling between Greece and Antioch, the center of the Seleucid Empire. Along with prosperity came improvements in the cultural areas. Ephesus became the center for the study of medicine and had a famous university established there.

The city was enclosed by a wall with a perimeter of four and a half miles. The walls were twenty-five feet high. Later, the kingdom of Pergamum governed the area, including Ephesus, and prosperity continued into Roman times. To assure a peaceful transition, the last king of Pergamum willed the entire empire to the Roman people in 133 BC.

In Roman times, Ephesus was not far behind Alexandria, Egypt, Antioch, and Syria in population and wealth. One of its famous distinctions came from its library of over 200,000 books. The library nearly overshadowed the library in Alexandria, Egypt, which claimed to be the largest library in the world. In 84 BC, Sulla attacked the city during one of the Roman civil wars. Nonetheless, prosperity continued under Roman rule, and in 6 BC, it became the capital of the province of Asia.

The city had a large agora, or marketplace, which was built in 4 BC. This marketplace went from the harbor into the city proper. The way into the city had many carved columns along the way. In this last century BC, many monuments were built. Ephesus was considered to be the banking center of western Asia Minor.

In 246 BC, Ephesus, along with several other cities, set up a permanent fund to supply capital for various trade opportunities. The interest gained on the loan (yes, interest was charged even then) was used to buy grain and then distributed, for free, to the poor. A series of famines in previous years has alarmed the city officials due to the loss of workforce during these famines. This is probably the first example of massive welfare ever practiced, even though their motives were not as pristine as one would hope.

Our next interest in Ephesus comes in AD 53–57. On return home to Antioch, Paul, on his second missionary journey, passed through Ephesus. While there, Paul established the first Christian church in Ephesus. This church was established in the middle of every pagan religion in the known world.

Being the great trade city it was, Ephesus had become a distribution center for the commercial businesses shipping trade goods from the Orient to Europe. Caravans carried every kind of commodity. Because of its location at the land terminus of the great trade route, Ephesus became the home for representatives of many of the companies shipping trade goods in both directions. Along the docks of the port in Ephesus, huge warehouses were built to store the goods.

Each of the companies had their own native representatives who watched over their company's welfare. Most of these representatives were married and brought their families with them. Not only did they bring their families, but they also brought their entire households, including slaves, servants, and even their priests and priestesses. Members of like religions established places of worship and built temples for each of their gods. Every major form of idolatry was practiced in this area.

Some of these religions were extremely perverted. But as time went on, these religions were accepted by everyone, regardless of the perversions. All of the religions were idolatrous. Some were so depraved that practicing them was outlawed in some countries. For instance, the religion of Semiramis, or mother-goddess worship, was so gross that Cyrus, Xerxes, and other Medo-Persian kings banished its priests from their land and labored to root it out of their empires. The religion moved from place to place, and every place they went, they were chased out. Finally, they came to Asia Minor, where they found a secure retreat.

As mentioned before, mother-goddess worship was prevalent. Mother goddess had its origins in ancient Babylon, where it was established by Semiramis, the wife of Nimrod. Nimrod became the first "king" on the earth, setting himself up in a position that would elevate him to the level of God.

In the book of Genesis, Nimrod is said to be "a mighty hunter before the LORD" (Genesis 10:9, NKJV). Most students of Scripture misinterpret the term hunter, believing that it is used only to describe someone who is killing animals for meat. While true, he did kill animals to supply food for others, and he was revered for his skill, the term, as used here, speaks of Nimrod's desire for power. The praise he received boosted his ego to the point that he wanted to be a king. He did establish a kingdom and built great cities, one of which was Babylon. Ultimately, Nimrod wanted to become God, and "a mighty hunter before the LORD" refers to his desire to be the sovereign of all men, even before God, or to be God.

When Nimrod decided that he wanted to be God, he rationalized that if he could find a place high enough, he could climb into heaven and usurp the position of the Most High. In the ancient mindset, people believed there were three levels of the heavens. (We see this same mindset in 2 Corinthians 12:2 (KJV), where Paul wrote, "I knew a man in Christ above fourteen years ago, (whether in the body, I cannot tell; [...] God knoweth;) such an one caught up to the third heaven." We know now that Paul was speaking of himself being transported to heaven, where he was given a vision. The first level was where the ancient people saw the birds fly. They could easily get higher than this by climbing mountains. The second level was where the clouds and stars were. They had experienced being on a mountain and inside a cloud, but they had never had access to the third heaven. The third heaven, or third level, was the place where God lived.

Since there was no natural place of the necessary height to reach the third heaven, Nimrod rationalized that he could build an artificial mountain where he could easily *walk into heaven*. Therefore, Nimrod began to construct the Tower of Babel.

The noted Jewish historian Flavius Josephus wrote:

> Now it was Nimrod who excited them [the early people] to such an affront and contempt of God [...] he gradually turned his government into tyranny, seeing no other way of turning men from the fear of God [...] The multitudes were very ready to follow the determination of Nimrod [...], and they built a tower, neither sparing any pains, nor being in any way negligent about the work: and, by reason of the multitude of hands employed in it, it grew very high [...] The place wherein they built the tower is now called Babylon.
>
> *The Antiquities of the Jews*, book one, ca. 92–94 CE
> (hereinafter, brackets mine)

Of note is the fact that Nimrod had heard the account of how God destroyed ungodly men with the flood of Noah. He thought he was too smart to be caught in another flood, so he used burnt brick and laid them with tar so that his artificial mountain would be waterproof.

Of course, we know the end of that story!

Alexander Hislop, in his book *The Two Babylons*, wrote in detail how Babylonian religion developed around traditions concerning Nimrod and his wife, Semiramis, and her child, Tammuz.

Nimrod became so evil that he was killed by his great-great-uncle Shem, cut into pieces; the pieces were burned and then sent to the major cities as an example of the consequences of idolatry. Following Nimrod's death, which was greatly mourned by the Babylonians, his wife, Semiramis, claimed that he had become the sun god. Later, she found that she was pregnant, and when her son, Tammuz, was born, she claimed that he was their hero, Nimrod, reborn.

She evidently had heard the prophecy of the coming Messiah who was to be born of the seed of a woman. This was known from Genesis 3:15. She claimed that her son was supernaturally conceived and that he was *the promised Seed, the Savior*. In the religion that was developed, not only was the son worshipped, but the mother was as well! (We will see more of Tammuz later on in our study.)

LEFT...
SEMIRAMIS AND
TAMMUZ

RIGHT...
ARTEMIS/DIANA
GODDESS OF HUNTING,
WILD ANIMALS, AND
PROTECTOR OF FEMALES

LEFT...
CYBELE,
PHRYGIAN GODDESS

RIGHT...
DEVAKI OR YASHODA
WITH KRISHNA

This system of idolatry spread from Babylon and scattered over the face of the earth. As these idolators traveled, they took with them their worship of the mother and child and the various symbols concerned with their worship. Bearing this in mind, we see that the mother and child became the grand objects of worship. In ancient pictures, we see the mother goddess with her son in her arms. The symbolism has spread to the ends of the earth. In Egypt, the mother and son were worshiped under the names Isis and Osiris; in India as Isi and Iswara; in Asia Minor as Cybele and Deoius; in Rome as Fortuna and Jupiter; in Greece as Ceres and Pluto. The ancient Germans called her Hertha; the Scandinavians called her Disa; the Etruscans called her Nutria; she was known as Aphrodite to the Greeks and Diana to the Romans, Nana to the Sumerians, Devaki and Krishna, and even as Shing-moo, the holy mother of China depicted with a child in her arms. Regardless of where the mother goddess showed up, she was the goddess of evil.

The major feature of all these religious symbols is a picture of a mother and child with a halo around the heads of both mother and son; the halo represents the sun, which was a major part of a religion of fertility.

Other religions were established throughout the region. There was emperor worship, worship of Artemis, Astarte, Serapia, Tyche, Apollo, Zeus, Balaam, Asclepius, Meander, and many others.

It was into this mishmash of religions that the early church came. As we continue on, I will talk a bit more about the religions surrounding the early churches with more detail as to how the letters concern each, but for now, I would like to plant this seed in your mind: the seven churches of Asia Minor faced much the same conditions as the Christian church faces today. What was written to them still goes for us today.

The church in Ephesus was in direct competition with many of these pagan religions. The temple of Artemis was one of the Seven Wonders of the Ancient World. As I have mentioned before, Artemis was the Greek name for the mother goddess. Another Greek name for this mother goddess was Diana. This was a fertility religion and the major religion of Ephesus.

Another temple was built for the goddess Hestia, the fire goddess, who was the personification of the hearth, where an eternal fire was dedicated to the deity and was equated with the life of the city. The temple was called the *prytaneion*. Because there were no matches, flints, or other means to start fires in the antiquities, the Ephesians went to the temple with sticks from the "narthex" plant. These sticks would be lit from the *eternal fire* in the temple. These sticks would burn for hours allowing the carrier to return home and kindle their fires. Special attention was given to the temple fires to ensure they didn't go out, and daughters of well-known families were given the task of protecting them. They were called the curetiae, meaning the "virgins of Hestia." The street to this temple was named the Curetiae street. That fire has long since gone out! We see Jesus commenting on this in verse five. This is what the one who walked "among the seven golden lampstands" (Revelation 2:1, ESV) speaks of to those who daily walked beneath the lamps on the Arcadians, warning them that just as the eternal fire on the altar of Hestia could be extinguished, their lamp could be removed from its place.

The famous temple of Diana still has parts of it standing today and is an architectural masterpiece. The temple was built on marshy soil so that it would not be subject to earthquakes, predominant in the area, or be threatened by floods. To ensure that the foundations of this massive building would not be laid on shifting, unstable ground, they were underpinned with a layer of closely trodden charcoal and then with a layer of sheepskins with their fleeces unshorn. Therefore, the foundation was *floating*. The temple was 425 feet long, 225 feet wide, and 60 feet high. It had 127 columns, each constructed by a different king. Of these, sixty were carved with reliefs. The crowning marvel of the construction was the placement of the lentils on top of the columns. This was done by constructing a gently sloping ramp, which was used to haul the lentils to their positions. One of the huge stones would not be set properly, and the architect was debating suicide. He slept and had a dream that the goddess had visited him and urged him to live because she would herself lay that stone. The next morning the stone had settled into place merely because of its own weight. The other tales of this monument are enough to fill many books.

The temple of Diana was a magnificent structure. Temple worshippers were numbered in the thousands. The service of the temple was in the hands of a high priest, eunuch priests, three grades of priestesses, and a large number of temple prostitutes, both male and female. The worship services were a weird mixture of shouts, wailings, burning incense, and playing flutes. The worshippers worked themselves into frenzies and did the most shameful things that could happen. Both male and female prostitutes served in the performance of orgiastic rituals required by the religion. These were done to imitate the fertility of nature.

The temple was also an authorized asylum for criminals. Anyone who had committed a crime could flee to the temple, and if he reached it before being caught, he was given asylum for as long as he wished.

The first bank in the world functioned in this temple under the personal supervision of the high priest, and private citizens deposited monies there for safekeeping. It did so much business that it was called *the bank of Asia*.

In 29 BC, Augustus Caesar commanded that temples be built in honor of his father Nero and the emperor Domitian. The Romans allowed any religion to be practiced if, first, the people would worship their emperors.

There was a temple to Bes, a fertility god of the Middle East, a temple of Apollo, a temple of Serapis (the combined goddess and son, Isis and Osiris), the river god Cayster, and many lesser pagan gods.

Ephesus was architecturally superb. It had a theater that was 495 feet in diameter and held 25,000 people. This is the theater that is referred to in Acts, chapter nineteen. The main street, called the Marble Way, ran from the theater to the harbor and was 1,735 feet long and 70 feet wide; it was lined with columns, shops, a multitude of buildings and was illuminated at night. Most of the streets had perfect drainage systems. There was a gymnasium, a marketplace, and a famous library.

There was a huge stadium, and Paul's reference of fighting with beasts in 1 Corinthians 15:32 is probably a reference to an actual experience of the apostle when he was made a spectacle in this very stadium.

At the date of the New Testament, Ephesus was a prosperous commercial center and was the largest city of its day. Its streets were constantly crowded with travelers and merchants from all parts of the civilized world. As the harbor became increasingly unusable, however, the trade was gradually diverted to Smyrna, and the importance of Ephesus diminished proportionately.

Ephesus was a center for the study of the art of magic and was renowned all over the world for its charms, incantations, and books of magic, most sold for fabulous sums. Mysterious incantations, written on parchment, were worn as amulets and alleged to be protection from evil and danger. There were indications that black magic was practiced, and some practiced spiritism.

Renegade Jews were adept in mystic matters, and many people came to them for charms to carry with them to ward off evil spirits. When Paul came to Ephesus, it was with signs and wonders from God, which would appeal to these people. Even handkerchiefs and aprons that had touched Paul had a miraculous healing power imparted to them, and the Ephesians were awestruck by them. They acknowledged a supernatural power greater than their own magic, and those who accepted Jesus as Savior burned their books of magic in the marketplace (Acts 19:19).

One of the most lucrative Ephesian industries was the manufacture of small silver images of Diana and her shrine, for which a ready market was found all over Asia Minor. When Paul preached the gospel of Jesus Christ there, it became apparent that his preaching was affecting their market. Demetrius and other silversmiths aroused the entire city, seized Paul and his companions, dragged them off to the theater, and created such a disturbance that Paul advisedly left the city (Acts 19:24–41; 20:1).

On his second missionary journey, as Paul returned home, he established a church in Ephesus. Then other churches were started, and the seven churches of Asia became a circuit, which, when we get to the book of Revelation, had become representative of all the things that could go wrong in a church.

It is to these churches the book of Revelation was written, but it must be noted that conditions found there some 2,000 years ago still exist. We can see the same problems in the church today in our own area. We won't have to go very far to see them.

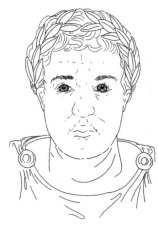

EUMENES II, KING OF PERGAMON, FROM 197–159 BC. HE WAS SON TO ATTALUS I SOTER AND QUEEN APOLLONIS. SURNAMED "SOTER" WHICH MEANS "SAVIOR." EUMENES II WAS KNOWN FOR UTILIZING PARCHMENT FOR MAKING BOOKS, WHEN THE SUPPLY OF PAPYRUS WAS PURPOSFULLY WITHHELD. THE LIBRARY AT PERGAMON RIVALED THE ALEXANDRIAN LIBRARY.

RIGHT...
TITUS FLAVIUS JOSEPHUS BORN 37–C. 100 YOSEF BEN MATITYAHU, A ROMANO-JEWISH HISTORIAN BORN TO A MATTHIAS III, A PRIEST, AND A ARISTOCRATIC MOTHER IN A ROYAL LINE OF THE HASMONEAN DYNASTY.

"To the angel of the church in Ephesus write: These things saith he that holdeth the seven stars in his right hand, he that walketh in the midst of the seven golden candlesticks" (verse one).

30

The first letter is addressed to the messenger of the church in Ephesus. John quotes Jesus as he begins the letter. He identifies Jesus as the author of the letter.

"I know thy works, and thy toil and patience, and that thou canst not bear evil men, and didst try them that call themselves apostles, and they are not, and didst find them false" (verse two).

Jesus begins His message by saying to the messenger of the church, "I know your works." At its inception, the church in Ephesus exhibited a spiritual vitality that came from its founder, Paul. He had a habit of going from house to house preaching, teaching, and warning the people of their errors.

Jesus knew how hard the people worked to spread the gospel message. The early church accomplished more widespread preaching of the gospel than the church ever has since.

The church in Ephesus hated evil, and they did everything they could to help men overcome their sinful natures by witnessing to them and telling them how they could be saved in Jesus Christ. This fervent evangelism is what got the church off to such a successful start. Even with our modern means of communication and travel, we have not been able to equal their evangelical success.

There were three major problems confronting the church in Ephesus: whenever the gospel was preached, it was not long before Judaizers appeared, trying to bring the converts back into the bondage of Jewish legalism. In addition, the church was faced with Gnostics and liberalism, which was preached by false teachers. In the normal course, the sophisticated Ephesian was accustomed to putting to the test what strangers said, even in secular things. The Christians in the church in Ephesus were not willing to accept any new doctrine unchallenged. So, when those came into the church claiming to be apostles, they applied the test for apostleship to them, found them lacking, and expelled them from their body.

The test for apostleship was rather simple. An apostle had to be either appointed by Jesus or by the other apostles. Every apostle had to have been present with Jesus during His earthly ministry.

"And thou hast patience and didst bear for my name's sake, and hast not grown weary" (verse three).

It is not without significance that "work," "labor," and "patience" are joined together in this letter. We see these same three things connected in 1 Thessalonians 1:3, but in that passage, they are qualified by the virtues of Christianity; Paul writes of "work of faith," "labor of love," and "patience of hope." The omission in the message to the church in Ephesus implies that faith, love, and hope had been lost to view and that their work was only a formality, the labor lifeless, and the patience uninspired. Christian work was once the willing evidence of loyalty to the Savior, and the desire to further advance His interests had become a form. The work, so gladly undertaken out of love for Him, had become a burden, and the patient endurance and constancy had become a wearisome continuance. Activities and consistency carried on, but the inspiration was gone, and enthusiasm had disappeared.

The Ephesians had a reputation for fickleness and instability, and everything was constantly in a state of change. Like the shifting site of the city and the shifting silt in the harbor, the attitude of the city was reflected in the church.

Service for Jesus Christ is a labor of love, but still, it is work, and no act of service is unnoticed by Jesus Christ. Even though we are not to "work" for any recompense, we are to do "good works." As we "work," we are not to grow weary. A Christian life should never be tiresome. If everyone in the body of Christ, even down to the local level, would each do their part, it would be joyful labor of love for everyone.

"But I have this against thee, that thou didst leave thy first love" (verse four).

About all I can say regarding this verse is that when I became a Christian, I couldn't get enough! From the words used here, we can see they hadn't entirely left their first love, but they were on their way. They had lost that intense and enthusiastic devotion to the person of Christ. The church had not only gotten off track in their doctrine but also in their personal relationship with Jesus Christ. Their toil, consistent performance, and undeviating orthodoxy had become formal obligations, without warmth or inspiration. The church had become like a car coasting downhill after the motor had conked out, without power, only moving under its own momentum. The bad thing about that is when you get to the bottom of the hill, you have nothing left to move you on. You are, as the phrase says, "dead in the water"!

"Remember therefore whence thou art fallen, and repent and do the first works; or else I come to thee, and will move thy candlestick out of its place, except thou repent" (verse five).

Do you remember when *you* first became a Christian?

What a thrill it was to know that Jesus loved me. Ann was saved before I was, and when we were first saved, we went everywhere to find something spiritual (going on). We would go anywhere at any time. I could not get enough! Guess what? I am still like that. I have a hard time understanding why every Christian isn't like that, but I see that down through the history of the church, men have left their first fervor for the Lord.

And repent! From what I have seen, Christians need to repent. Repentance means to get back with Jesus. People don't want to hear that they are not the holy, pious saints they think they are. When anything gets in the way of an individual's relationship with Jesus, we had better repent.

In the church in Ephesus, the congregation had begun to go astray. They needed to remember how it was before they were saved and what salvation had brought them. In Paul's letter to the Ephesians, he wrote them:

"You were dead in your trespasses [...], but you have been made alive in Christ" (Ephesians 2:1, paraphrased).

"By His grace are ye saved" (Ephesians 2:8, paraphrased).

"You have the promise of sitting with him in the heavenlies" (Ephesians 2:6, paraphrased).

"You were once called the uncircumcision by the Jews" (Ephesians 2:11, paraphrased).

"You were separated from Christ; you were alienated from Israel; you were without hope; you were without God" (Ephesians 2:12, paraphrased).

"You were brought close by the blood of Christ" (Ephesians 2:13, paraphrased).

"You are no longer strangers and sojourners, but fellow-citizens with the saints and the household of God" (Ephesians 2:19, paraphrased).

"You are the inhabitation of God" (Ephesians 2:22, paraphrased).

"You are the joint heirs and fellow members and fellow partakers of the promise of Christ" (Ephesians 3:6, paraphrased).

It's obvious that something had gone wrong, but what? In order to see what had happened, we turned to Paul's letter to the Ephesians. There we see a list of the things the congregation there were doing right and the things they were doing wrong.

I have compiled a list of both. The good things they were doing:

1. They were showing love toward fellow citizens (Ephesians 1:15).
2. They had faith in the Lord (Ephesians 1:15).

The bad things they were doing:

Ephesians 4:31–32
1. Bitterness
2. Wrath
3. Anger
4. Clamor
5. Railing
6. Maliciousness
7. Hard-heartedness
8. Unforgiveness

Ephesians 5:9, 31
9. Fornication

10. Filthiness
11. Foolishness
12. Being unwise
13. Drinking
14. Wives were not in submission to their husbands
15. Husbands were not loving
16. Husbands were "mama's boys" and kept going back home

Ephesians 6:1, 4, 5, 9
17. Children were disobedient to their parents
18. Children were physically and verbally abused
19. Slaves were disobedient
20. Slave owners were cruel

The church needs to get back to that first love. We must never let anything get in the way of our relationship with Jesus. That includes family, friends, social or recreational events. There is a thing called a calendar, which shows us the days of the week. "Our worship service is always on Sunday." "The church building is always right there." "Wednesday night prayer meeting is always on Wednesday." The church never leaves its foundation. Since this is true, why isn't every member in church when the doors open?

The penalty for not honoring your Savior is that Jesus will shut down your church! I can take you for a ride right now and show you a number of churches that are either boarded up or being used for some other purpose than worship. Once they were thriving churches with large congregations, but the crowds don't come anymore because, in many churches, the Word of God is not preached.

When we see Jesus making a comment on the city of Ephesus in verse one, "The one who walked among the seven golden lampstands" of the church, He uses a local landmark to teach them that just as the "eternal fire" on the altar of Hestia could be extinguished (verse five), so could their lamp be removed from its place.

Jesus is watching us as He watched the church in Ephesus. If the candlestick isn't sending out light, He will snuff it out. Today there is no church in Ephesus. In fact, there is no Ephesus.

"But this thou hast, that thou hatest the works of Nicolaitans, which I also hate" (verse six).

It seems that in the early days of the church, there was a movement to bring the priesthood of the Mosaic law into the church. Priests had been supported and even pampered by the Jews, and the church didn't have a priesthood. Evidently, there was a movement to set up a hierarchy in the church.

This is an unscriptural idea that causes the members of the church to be enslaved to a human or humans who determine the doctrine. This is a dangerous principle since every Christian is dependent on a relationship with Jesus Christ and is personally responsible for the spiritual vitality of that relationship.

This leads us to the Nicolaitans! The word "Nicolaitans" comes from two Greek words, nikos and laos. *Nikos* means "to conquer" or "to place in a position of subservience." *Laos* means "the people." These Nicolaitans had come into the church with an agenda. They wanted to be the boss. They wanted to set the guidelines for the operation of the church. They wanted to put their practices in place so that the church would rely on men for the solutions to their problems and not rely on God. They wanted a priesthood like the other religions in Ephesus. It is this "work" that Jesus hated.

It is interesting to note that in the New Testament, there are only two mentions of Jesus hating anything, but here in verse six, and later in verse fifteen, Nicolaism, which is synonymous with a modern-day ecclesiasticism, is a concept of which Jesus said, "I hate!" This is an extremely bad thing for the church—for Jesus to hate it so much. Why?

When men get control of the spiritual training of other people and are in a position to dominate the church, their theological position will eventually dominate that church. When that church is dominated, they will formulate their own doctrine at the expense of Scripture.

You can always identify present-day "Nicolaitans" by the structure of their hierarchy. There will be popes, archbishops, bishops, cardinals, district superintendents, and other titles. Each of these is a position of domination over the members of the church. In comparison, the only biblical leaders in the church are elders, deacons, deaconesses, and pastors.

Can you even imagine hearing Jesus say that He hates the doctrine and teaching of our church? That is why I keep saying I have no axe to grind and my opinion is worth nothing. The only authority of this church is the teachings as recorded in God's holy Word, the Bible. Changing these teachings will certainly bring the wrath of God when He sets up His kingdom!

"He that hath an ear, let him hear what the Spirit saith to the churches. To him that overcometh, to him will I give to eat of the tree of life, which is in the Paradise of God" (verse seven).

This is an expression of the Lord Jesus Christ that appears in many of His parables. This statement implies three kinds of individuals:

1. Those without ears. This, of course, doesn't refer to physical ears. He is obviously referring to those who are not attuned to the Holy Spirit through the new birth; that is, they have not been born again and thus are not anointed with the Holy Spirit. Consequently, they cannot hear God when He speaks.
2. Those who are dull of hearing. Not all born-again Christians are willing to hear the Holy Spirit when He speaks. The Holy Spirit upbraided the Hebrew Christians for being "dull of hearing" (Hebrews 5:11).
3. There are those spiritually-minded Christians, who are willing to hear what the Holy Spirit says, but the test of the person hearing the message is seen in his subsequent conduct, for we are taught that we should be "doers of the Word, and not hearers only" (James 1:22).

I will comment on those who "have ears" at the end of chapter three, for Jesus uses these same words to all seven churches of Asia.

Overcoming the world is the experience that takes place in the life of the individual who puts forth his or her faith in Jesus Christ. There is no other way men can become overcomers. The tree of life is the tree that gives eternal life. This is the tree that is in the middle of the paradise of God. We will see more of this tree in chapter twenty-two.

The Church in Smyrna

The name *Smyrna* means "bitter." *Smyrna* is the proper Greek word that is translated into the English word "myrrh." Smyrna is an aromatic resin from the Burseraceae family, and its botanical name is *Commiphora Myrrh*. This resin has been used from remote ages as an ingredient in incense, perfumes, and in the holy oil of the Jews for embalming. This resin comes from a bush that does not grow more than nine feet in height, but it is sturdy with knotty branches, which stand out at right angles to the trunk and end in a sharp spine.

Smyrna is scantily found in an area that is so dry and bare that it is called Tehama, meaning "hell." Smyrna comes chiefly from the Arabian Peninsula. In addition to making perfume, smyrna was used as a type of narcotic, which deadened the senses somewhat, allowing the taker to withstand intense pain. The plant named myrrh today is different from the biblical plant but is sold by the milligram. You can purchase it over the internet in 550 mg capsules, at $8.99 per one hundred. Today's myrrh is used to treat ulcers in the mouth, but it is so bitter it is rarely used in the United States.

Smyrna (the resin) is mentioned three times in the New Testament. The first time is in Matthew, chapter two, when the three wise men come from the east, bringing their treasures of gold, frankincense, and smyrna. The second time is seen in the Gospel of Mark at the crucifixion of our Lord. He was offered wine mixed with smyrna in order to help alleviate, anesthetically, the suffering He bore. The third place is in John, chapter nineteen. When Jesus died, Nicodemus came with Joseph of Arimathea, and the two men, after carefully taking the body of Jesus down from the cross, wrapped it in a long linen cloth, and in the folds of the cloth, they placed a hundred-pound weight of aloes and smyrna. In each of these incidents, the word is translated as "myrrh."

The city received its name from the trade of smyrna. It was the seaport of the fragrance and perfume of myrrh. In the book of Revelation, smyrna came to symbolize the story of the Asian church when it entered a terrible period of persecution. Smyrna pictures suffering and was used in the embalming of the dead. Smyrna typifies the suffering of our Lord for our sins.

Smyrna is one of the ancient cities of the world. It was a great city with a population of over 100,000, and its harbor was one of the finest in the world. The gulf of Smyrna reaches back inland about thirty miles. It is beautiful and spacious. The gulf of Smyrna is L-shaped and enters from the north.

The entrance to the gulf is formed by the Melaena promontory to the west and on the east by a projection of land where the ancient city Phocaea stood.

The city of the New Testament was the third city on the site. The original was little more than a collection of the citadel and a smattering of houses. The Lydians attacked the city and destroyed it. They, in turn, rebuilt it after 300 years had passed. The city degenerated to not much more than dust, and in the fourth century BC, an attempt was made to revive the ancient city. Antigonus began the task, and Alexander the Great intervened with the same goal in mind. As had been mentioned before, Alexander's general, Lysimachus, followed Alexander's orders and completed the rebuilding of the well-planned city, which came to be known as the "Flower of Ionia." It flourished economically, commercially, and extending its rapidly growing boundaries, developed into one of the most prosperous cities of the then-known world.

From Smyrna, there was access to the Hermus River valley at the interior of the province of Lydia. Although Smyrna's harbor was superior to that of Ephesus, it looked to the northwest. Ships from the south would therefore be more likely to put in Ephesus and avoid the trip around the Chios and Melaena promontories, everything coming from the northern Aegean Sea, by nature, funneled into Smyrna.

Smyrna was also located on one of the legs of the famous Royal Road and fed into the great trade route to the interior of Asia Minor and the Orient. Like Ephesus, it was a major city of commerce. It was located just thirty-five miles north of Ephesus, and like Ephesus, it was filled with the pagan temples of Apollo, Asclepius, Cybele, Zeus, and Emperor Tiberius.

When Smyrna came under the control of the Romans in 27 BC, it had already proved itself as a faithful ally to Rome. The city flourished under Roman dominance.

Pagan religion dominated the Smyrna skyline. Mount Pagus, which rose some 500 feet above the harbor, was topped with an acropolis, or fortress. Around this fortress curved a "street of gold." Pagan shrines were erected at both ends. One was for the mother goddess Cybele, and the other for Zeus, the chief god of Greece.

Along this "golden street" were other shrines: a shrine to Asclepius, Demeter, and Dionysus. There were also shrines to many other lesser-known gods of the Smyrnans. Smyrna existed as a self-sufficient city whose deities were thought to be the source of its success.

Smyrna was a great political center, and it was always on the winning side. The city never lost a cause. It was always right! The conquering Romans made Smyrna a free city with its own government. It was the proudest of all of the cities of Asia Minor. For them, God was not supreme. The emperor of Rome was their god.

Rome was lenient to their concepts of religions. A citizen of Rome could worship any god they wished, but with an exception: mandatory emperor worship was imposed, with the threat of death for disobedience. Annually, every person was required to burn incense on the altar of Caesar and sign a written acknowledgment they had done so. This was an official Roman document that had to be witnessed by a magistrate.

One such certificate reads as follows:

> To those who have been appointed to preside over sacrifices, from Inokeskeus, from the village of Theoxenis, together with his children, Aias and Heva, who reside in the village of the Theadelphia. We have always sacrificed to the gods, and now in your presence, according to the regulations, we have sacrificed and offered libations, and tasted the sacred things, and we ask that you give us a certification that we have done so. May you fare well.
>
> Barclay, *Letters to the Seven Churches*, 18

Signatures of all three were added.

Then there was an addendum: "We, the representatives of the Emperor, Serenos and Hermas, have seen you sacrificing." The magistrates added their signatures to this document.

To Smyrna, worldly things were the first and last. To Smyrna, the first and the last were glories of Greek culture. Alexander the Great wanted to make it a model city, and after his death, Lysimachus, one of his generals, built it into a model city. Its streets were wide and spacious.

In what was considered to be one of the most beautiful in the world, the inhabitants were encouraged to take pride in their city and themselves. In spring and summer, the entire city was bedecked with garlands of flowers, and the people wore crowns of laurel leaves and flowers and danced in the city streets in celebration.

The primary religion was that of mother-goddess worship. She was worshipped as the goddess of nature. Her worship was universal in Phrygia and was wild and unrestrained. She was known as the "giver of wealth" and was worshipped with drums, symbols, horns, and her followers danced orgiastic dances. As with the fertility rites of the usual nature, or fertility religions, the worship of this pagan deity was accomplished with sacred prostitution and consecrated license, in which many Christians had indulged in their unregenerate days and that still tempted them.

The fertility goddess Cybele was said to be as the seasons of nature. She was the goddess of corn, and her chief festival was at harvest time. The priests were termed *stephanophori* in reference to the laurel or golden crowns they wore in public processions. As such, she was said to be carried off to the underworld each fall by Pluto to die, as the plants die in winter. She would be reborn in the spring and then be released to make the fields fertile once more.

The letter to the church in Smyrna is filled with the sorrow of suffering and contains a message for the church in all generations as it passes through trials and tribulations. So far as this letter is concerned, suffering and persecution are ever the lot of God's people in every generation.

Jesus Christ's letter to the church in Smyrna begins:

"And to the angel of the church in Smyrna write: These things saith the first and the last, who was dead, and lived again" (verse eight).

As in the letter to the church in Ephesus, this letter is addressed to the "angel" of the church in Smyrna. Again, the "angel" is the messenger of the church, or its pastor. Jesus identifies Himself as the "Alpha and Omega," the beginning and the end, or the eternal God in the flesh, who was crucified, buried, and resurrected.

His revealing of Himself must have been a strong appeal to the believers in Smyrna. As we will see, the animosity of their pagan neighbors and the ruthless, unyielding attitude of the Roman administrators rendered it almost inevitable that many of these Christians would ultimately pay the supreme penalty of death. But that was not the end! And herein lay the inspiration of Jesus' words: He had died at the hands of men, as they may be called on to do, *but He lived again!*

But these words had a more intimate significance to the Christians of Smyrna. Their patron deity was the mother goddess Cybele, whose worship was based on her death in the fall and her symbolic resurrection to a new life in the spring. Using the very mythology of the people to whom He was writing, Jesus plainly indicated that these mythical events were only the imaginations of men and that He was the only One who had actually descended into death and risen in resurrection power.

Cybele was only a shadow. He was the substance. In the Greek text, Jesus uses the aorist tense, which makes it clear that the reference was the *only* act of resurrection. For the followers of Cybele, the story was repeated every year, but Jesus descended into death and was resurrected forever!

Not only was Jesus appealing to religion, but this was also a commentary on the history of Smyrna. As I have said before, Sardis was captured by the Lydians and was so devastatingly humiliated by them that, for centuries, their name was removed from the role of cities. The city had been almost wiped out by earthquakes, and each time, it was revived. It had, on three occasions, become dead and lived again.

These historical experiences were only shadows of a far greater reality, and Jesus assumed the place of fulfillment of them all. He had died and lived again! There was no doubt about the implication! Jesus was declaring the falsity of heretical religions.

"I know thy tribulation, and thy poverty (but they art rich), and the blasphemy of them that say that they are Jews, and they are not, but are a synagogue of Satan" (verse nine).

The clash between the all-powerful Roman Empire and the church was inevitable. Rome was tolerant of all religions that did not forbid participation in the cult-of-emperor worship.

Obviously, the Christian church could not take part in this type of idolatry, and sooner or later, the Roman authority would take notice of their failure to obey the declarations of the empire. In Smyrna, the day came sooner rather than later. The church was persecuted, and at times, in almost unparalleled ways in history.

Failure to obey the Romans cost the Christians loss of jobs, properties, and businesses. Their possessions were spoiled; property was confiscated. Informers were paid rewards for turning them in. They became poverty-stricken.

But the spoiling of their goods did not escape the eyes of the Master, and He declares that He knows their poverty (literally their destitution), but He adds paradoxically that they are rich. Stripped of their material possessions, they were enriched in all spiritual treasures of eternity. Their eternal wealth was beyond earthly comparison.

The lot of these Christians was worsened still further by the opposition of the Jews who lived in Smyrna; many acted as informers against them. Jesus says that they are not Jews but are of a "synagogue of Satan." In Jesus' eyes, they were not true Jews but were an emissary of the prime enemy of God and His people, the devil. Jesus regarded their rejection of their Messiah as a sham, and He considered them hypocrites. They had turned against His church and harassed His followers.

The Jews' former position and nearness to God only amplified the present distance from Him. Their synagogue was not of God but of the devil. In their present state, they were viewed as inspired by Satan.

Fear not the things which thou art about to suffer: behold, the devil is about to cast some of you into prison, that ye may be tried; And ye shall have tribulation ten days. Be thou faithful unto death, and I will give thee the crown of life.

Verse ten

For the church in Smyrna, the storm clouds were gathering. The savage cruelty of Rome was about to wreak its vengeance on the inoffensive Christians, but the power of the devil who instigated it was strictly limited. The devil's activities are always subject to the permissive will of God, and he cannot touch God's people without permission, and even the feeblest Christian is protected by the stronger power of God. Testing and trial may be allowed by God, but its extent is always determined by God's purpose. Jesus says, "Fear not." The time of trouble would produce its own strength, and the Christians need not be frightened or intimidated.

While enemies of flesh and blood were responsible for the physical attacks, the cause of them was the sheer hatred of the devil for God and His people. Jesus assured the Christians in Smyrna that the period of trial was limited to ten days, indicating that there was a limit beyond which the wrath of man and the bitterness of Satan are not allowed to go. We are never tried beyond the endurance God gives us in times of trial.

We are never tried beyond the strength God gives us at the period; in all circumstances, His grace is sufficient.

Some of the members of the church in Smyrna were appalled by the threatened torture and possible death, denied their Lord, and paid tribute to Caesar. It was very easy to escape poverty, jail, and death. All you had to do was take a pinch of incense, burn it on an altar of Caesar, and fill out a form. Then you were back in the graces of the Roman Empire. It was very tempting to avoid persecution and trouble by taking the easy way out. Yet, Jesus assured those who would endure that He would give them the "crown of life," even if they were killed.

As the citizens of Rome had been faithful, even unto death, Jesus challenged His people to be faithful unto death. It costs to be loyal to Jesus Christ, and He has the right to demand our loyalty.

The reference to a crown had a definite significance. The public buildings that encircled the hill of Pagos were commonly referred to as the "crown of Smyrna." The citizens boasted so much of the beauty of this "crown" that Apollonius of Tyana advised them to be occupied with their own character than the glory of their city and said,

> It is a greater charm to wear a crown of men than a crown of porticoes and pictures and gold, for buildings are seen only in their place, but men are seen everywhere and spoken of everywhere.
> Apollonius of Tyana (ca. AD 15–100)

The crown was a common topic of the city.

The Christian who was faithful to Jesus was promised an immortal crown. Jesus promised no fading laurel wreath and no earthly crown of glory but the victor's crown, which is eternal life!

"He that hath an ear, let him hear what the Spirit saith unto the churches. He that overcometh shall be shall not be hurt of the second death" (verse eleven).

Finally, Jesus tells the Christians in Smyrna, as He told the Christians in Ephesus, to "tune in spiritually," to listen closely to the words of this letter. What follows is extremely important: "If you can resist following the rest of the world, and if you can be faithful, *in spite of all that can happen*, you will live with Christ for eternity and not spend eternity in the lake of fire. This is the second death!"

The Church in Pergamum

Pergamum is a beautiful and illustrious city. It was the capital of Asia Minor. Its origins are obscure, but there is evidence that it was occupied during the Stone and Bronze Ages. Human habitation began in Pergamum around 800 BC, but Pergamum's period of glory did not begin until Hellenistic times. Following the death of Alexander the Great, his empire was divided between his four generals. Lysimachus received western Asia Minor. At the time, he came into possession of 9,000 talents, a huge treasure derived from Alexander's extensive conquests.

Lysimachus placed a part of his money in Pergamum under the care of a eunuch named Philetaerus. In 281 BC, Lysimachus died in a battle and left no heir. Although most of his territory came under the control of Antiochus, Philetaerus, in firm control of Pergamum, the treasure of Lysimachus, became the undisputed ruler of the city.

Philetaerus was an intelligent, diplomatic ruler, and he maintained good relations with neighboring cities and began the beautification of the city, preparing a favorable political climate.

When he died in 263 BC, his nephew and adopted son, Eumenes I, succeeded him. Usually called the first king of Pergamum, Eumenes did little of note to further the city, and when he died in 241 BC, his successor, Attalus I, found some large problems facing him. The Gauls, a fierce tribe of semibarbaric warriors who had recently arrived in Asia Minor, were causing havoc in the neighboring kingdoms, and both Philetaerus and Eumenes had felt it wise to pay their extortion demands. Attalus I thought himself strong enough to refuse them, and war was the result. A great battle took place in 230 BC, and Attalus defeated the Gauls. He then found a new ally in Rome, and a strong bond was formed between the two cities. Attalus died, and Eumenes II acceded to the throne. He profited from the goodwill of the Romans, who had avoided war in this area. They were eventually forced into a war with Antiochus the Great from Syria, and the Roman defeat of Antiochus left the Romans with his territory.

They had no desire to administer it themselves, so they gave it all to Eumenes. Now Pergamum was at its highest point. A great building program was initiated, and the city soon had many new buildings and works of art. Pergamum developed into one of the foremost cities of the Mediterranean.

Eumenes died in 159 BC, and his brother, Attalus II, ascended to the throne of Pergamum. His reign was also in partnership with Rome. Attalus was attacked by Prusias of Bithynia in a war that dragged on for years. It finally ended when Roman troops arrived in 154 BC. In 146 BC, Rome attacked the city of Corinth as an example to the other Greek cities. Attalus sent troops to help the Romans, and Corinth fell.

Attalus III became king when his uncle died in 138 BC. He was a strange man who was disliked by his subjects. He ruled only three years and left one of the most famous wills ever seen in the world. He willed Pergamum to Rome.

Only once did the old pride of the royal city lift itself to revolt against the Romans. In 88 BC, Mithridates, the king of Pontus, fought against the Romans to free the citizens. The people joined him and killed the Romans living in the city, but the campaign led by the Roman general, Sulla, succeeded in driving out Mithridates, and Pergamum returned to its old ally Rome once again.

Important and beautiful buildings began to rise in Pergamum. The upper city was occupied by the royal family, and here stood the palace of Eumenes II, as well as that of Attalus I. North of these palaces were barracks for the soldiers, a command tower, and arsenals. The most spectacular monument of the upper city was the high narrow theater, in front of which was a long terrace with a colonnade ending in the north with a temple to Dionysus. Behind the theater was a temple to Athena. The colonnade on the north joined the famous library.

Both Eumenes and Attalus were great book collectors and, during their reigns, amassed a large library. There was also a huge library in Alexandria, Egypt. Ptolemy became jealous of the library in Pergamum. This jealousy brought about an unexpected benefit for the entire world. Up to this time, all ancient writings were put on scrolls made of papyrus. Papyrus grew best in Egypt along the Nile and could hardly be obtained elsewhere. Ptolemy, determined to out-collect Eumenes, forbade the export of papyrus and forced Eumenes to find another medium on which to write. Among the materials tested were the skins of animals of which sheepskin came to be the most desirable. The skins were scraped until they were very thin and subtle and came to be known as "parchment," the English word for the material that is derived from the name Pergamum.

There was one major difference between papyrus and parchment. Papyrus could be made into long pieces and rolled into scrolls. Parchment could not. Because of this, parchment was cut into sheets and sewn together at one edge, with the pages opening from right to left, or vice versa. This formed what is called a "codex." This codex was the forerunner of our modern bound books.

With this advancement, the library in Pergamum grew and, as a result, became a center of learning, and many princes, priests, and scholars came there to study.

Just as commercial travel had brought religions from all over the world to Ephesus, with this influx of students from all over the world came their religions to Pergamum. Eventually, Pergamum became noted for its many and varied pagan religions, complete with pagan temples to the pagan gods.

"And to the angel of the church in Pergamum write: These things saith he that hath the sharp two-edged sword" (verse twelve).

Jesus reveals Himself in verse twelve as "He who hath the sharp two-edged sword." This refers to God's word of judgment. "For the word of God is living, and active, and sharper than any two-edged sword, and piercing even to the dividing of soul and spirit, of both joints and marrow, and quick to discern the thoughts and intents of the heart" (Hebrews 4:12). Jesus is telling the messenger of the church in Pergamum that nothing escapes His sight. All are naked to His eyes; there is nothing that we can hide from Him. Because of this, we should be aware of how we live our Christian lives. He is the One who will judge all men righteously. God's judgment is not to be taken lightly. It is an eternal matter.

Jesus commanded those Christians at the church in Pergamum who had stayed faithful to Him in view of all of the pressures and conditions they were facing each day. All around them were all of the evils of man to man, and even those subjected to those evils stayed faithful to Him.

> I know where thou dwellest, even where Satan's throne is; and thou holdest fast my name, and thou didst not deny my faith, even in the days of Antipas my witness, my faithful one, who was killed among you where Satan dwelleth.
>
> Verse thirteen

Jesus is referring to the fact that these Christians live where Satan has great authority and great power. What is Satan's throne?

In the city, at one end of the main street, there was a temple dedicated to the pagan goddess of Athens, Athena. At the other end was a temple dedicated to the chief Greek savior, the god

Zeus. In between were altars to every pagan god or idol known to man. Among them were Dionysus, the wine god, and Asclepius, the god of healing. There were three other temples dedicated to the Roman emperor worship.

A medical school was attached to a cult that worshiped the sun. The Greek and Roman name for this god was Titan; the Asian name for this god was "Asclepius," or the "man-instructing serpent," whom we know as Satan or the devil. This refers to the fact that the serpent that "opened the eyes of Adam and Eve" was the one who gave them knowledge of good and evil. The snake was a symbol of this religion.

According to the fundamental doctrine of this cult, the "sun god" was the one and only god Titan. Notice the sound, [teitan]. Sounds like Satan, doesn't it?

In the temple to Asclepius, the floors were literally crawling with snakes. There were snakes of all kinds, and these snakes, worshipped as gods, were protected and multiplied to the point that they were underfoot throughout the city. If you remember, Nimrod was killed and cut up; the pieces were burned and sent around to the cities to show what happens to those who insist on being evil. Well, this "great god of Babylon" was pictured as a tree, stripped of its branches, and cut down to the ground, leaving only a stump. But the serpent, or Satan, is shown wrapped around the stump from which sprouts another tree of a different kind, which is destined never to be cut down. Thus, Nimrod, deified as the sun god, comes to life again by the power of the serpent, Asclepius. Thus, the serpent, or snake, was considered to be a healer. As such, snakes were used in the Aesculapium (hospital) as cures for diseases and ills of all kinds.

For instance, snakes were used in the treatment of mental disorders. In the temple, there was a long tunnel, dark inside, with holes in the walls. The person with the mental disorder was made to walk through the tunnel. As he or she walked, the snakes would slither around his or her feet, and "doctors," stationed at the holes, would whisper suggestions to the patient. What they said was not documented, but many were cured by this "shock treatment," and those healed were spoken of all over the world. Less advertised were the patients who were killed by snake bites or those who went stark raving mad.

The symbol of Asclepius is a staff with snakes entwined. By the way, this is the symbol of the medical profession today. This religion was another aspect of the one started by Semiramis, the wife of Nimrod.

As discussed before, the religions of Semiramis were harried out of Persia, and eventually, the religions found a safe haven in Pergamum. This temple is what Jesus calls "Satan's throne." As time and the early glory of Pergamum passed, the worship of Satan continued.

Ephesians 2:2 calls Satan "the god of this age." First Peter 5:8 describes Satan as a "roaring lion [...] seeking whom he may devour." And Satan set up his operations in the center of learning and the healing arts and made his home in Pergamum. Combining these arts, he set out to command people's minds through the education system, healing their ills, and controlling their souls through the pagan religions.

Satan's reign in Asia Minor proved to be highly visible. Smyrna housed the "Synagogue of Satan," Thyatira hosted one of Satan's schools, and Pergamum became the site of the throne of Satan, and because of its intense evil, was known by Jesus as "Satan's home." A secondary reference to Satan's throne was because Pergamum was the center of idolatrous worship in the world.

In reference to Antipas, he was a man who refused to be involved in emperor worship. He was put to death by being slowly roasted in a brass bull. Ever since, Antipas has been honored as a martyr whose life has been an example of perseverance for Jesus Christ. Jesus describes him as a "faithful witness." He died because of his witness to the truth of God.

Today, in the Middle East, we see the same evil being promoted. In my opinion, Satan's throne is still in existence in the same general area. The religions of Babylon are rampant throughout the Arab nations.

> But I have a few things against thee, because thou hast there some that hold the teaching of Balaam, who taught Balak to cast a stumblingblock before the children of Israel, to eat things sacrificed to idols, and to commit fornication.
>
> Verse fourteen

In the church in Pergamum, there were those who held to the teachings of Balaam. This is the Balaam of Numbers, chapters twenty-two to twenty-five. Balaam struggled between being true to God's Word and his desire for honor among men. King Balak diagnosed his problem, "I said I would reward you handsomely, but the LORD has kept you from being rewarded" (Numbers 24:11, NIV).

Balaam wanted the riches of life so badly that he instructed Balak how to cause the Jews to bring a curse on themselves.

> Behold, these caused the children of Israel, through the counsel of Balaam, to commit trespass against Jehovah in the matter of Peor, and so the plague was among the congregation of Jehovah.
>
> Numbers 31:16

> And Israel abode in Shittim; and the people began to play the harlot with the daughters of Moab: for they called the people unto the sacrifices of their gods; and the people did eat, and bowed down to their gods. And Israel joined himself unto Baal-Peor: and the anger of Jehovah was kindled against Israel. And Jehovah said unto Moses, Take all the chiefs of the people, and hang them up unto Jehovah before the sun, that the fierce anger of Jehovah may turn away from Israel. And Moses said unto the judges of Israel, Slay every one of his men that have joined themselves unto Baal-Peor.
>
> Numbers 25:1–5

Men like Balaam existed in the first-century church too. Jude 4:10–11 says that men rushed into Balaam's error for profit. These men prove that Jesus said: "No man can serve two masters; For either he will hate the one and love the other; Or else he will hold to one, and despise the other. Ye cannot serve God and mammon" (Matthew 6:24).

If the pattern held true, the Balaamites compromised the message of Jesus Christ just as the Balaam of old in their quest to entice them with immorality and the lifestyle of idolators.

"So hast thou also some that hold the teaching of the Nicolaitans in like manner" (verse fifteen).

Another group of compromising people had infiltrated the church fellowship. These were the same group of people who had infiltrated the church in Ephesus. They were called Nicolaitans. We have discussed this thoroughly in our study of the letter to the church in Ephesus. In the letter to the church in Ephesus, Jesus says He hates the "works," or deeds of the Nicolaitans; now He says that He hates the teachings of the Nicolaitans. Like those who preached the doctrine of Baalam, these people sought honor among men, but they went one step farther and set themselves up to rule over the church.

This movement rose up from a class of people who looked to be exalted over the great mass of people. They alone had the power to interpret and to mediate the Word and the will of God. They had the power to forgive sins and to excommunicate. They not only infiltrated the church but also entered the political, imperial, and governmental arena of the world. So, both the church and the government became pawns in a game of political power, and the two were "married" together. The doctrine of the Nicolations began early, but by the time we see them in the book of Revelation, their deeds had become a system and a theology.

Priestcraft supplanted the preacher of the Word of God. Ceremony took the place of the regenerating power of the Holy Spirit, and the church opened its heart to the love of power and the world. All of these things came to pass in the church in Pergamum about AD 300. The class distinction between clergy and laity grew even wider and wider. The assembly was no longer a company of believers, of saved, regenerated souls, but a channel through which sacramental and hypothetical salvation was offered.

In the Old Testament (Exodus 19:5–6), the Lord said,

> Now therefore, if ye will obey my voice indeed, and keep my covenant, then ye shall be mine own possession from among all peoples: for all the earth is mine: and ye shall be unto me a kingdom of priests, and a holy nation. These are the words which thou shalt speak unto the children of Israel.

What was offered to the Jews was actually realized in the Christian assembly. Everyone became a priest of God!

Peter named two things that forever undermined priestcraft and salvation by ritual and ceremony: "Ye also, as living stones, are built up a spiritual house, to be a holy priesthood, to offer up spiritual sacrifices, acceptable to God through Jesus Christ" (1 Peter 2:5). The old day of the priest is gone. The veil covering the Holy of Holies in the Jewish temple was torn from the top to the bottom when Jesus died on the cross, making it possible for all Christians to enter the Holy of Holies without a human intercessor, and any Christian can go to God in prayer for himself or herself as a member of the holy priesthood given to us through Jesus Christ. That is the true Christian faith, but in the short time of 300 years after this letter was written, the church was led into ceremonialism. Gone were all of the spiritual liberties and endowments of the Christian fellowship. Salvation by ritual had replaced salvation through the sacrifice of Jesus Christ, and the mother-goddess religion was introduced into the church through compromise.

This isn't an ancient story but a monstrous system of error that girdles the globe to this day and to this minute. The Lord Jesus Christ hates their doctrine of sacramental salvation. This religion is modern-day Roman Catholicism! The opposition to Jesus Christ and His truth is from within the church now, instead of from outside. We will see that this church is part of the religious system referred to as the "MYSTERY, BABYLON THE GREAT, THE MOTHER OF THE HARLOTS AND OF THE ABOMINATIONS OF THE EARTH" in Revelation 17:5.

"Repent therefore; or else I come to thee quickly, and I will make you make war against them with the sword of my mouth" (verse sixteen).

Since compromise entered into the church, Jesus launches His counterattack. He tells them, "Repent!" To repent means to stop doing what you are doing and do a 180-degree turn. This is exactly what the Bible tells us over and over. The church must turn away from ungodly worship and ungodly living and take up a holy passion for purity.

Jesus lays out the options: "Repent, or else!" At first glance, the consequence of disobedience doesn't sound too bad: "I will come to you." We want Jesus to come to us but not to make war against us. A premature coming of Jesus spells trouble. His coming would be with His sharp, two-edged sword to clean up the church, just as he cleaned out the Temple.

Roman governors were divided into two classes: those who had the "right of the sword" and those who did not. Those who had this right also had the power over life and death.

The proconsul of Pergamum had this right and could use it at will against Christians. Jesus reminds the church that it would be better to experience the sword of the proconsul than to face the sword of His mouth because the sword of the proconsul was temporary, while His was eternal.

As with other churches, Jesus calls on the members to listen closely to His words. He has already given overcomers the promise to eat from the tree of life, to be given the crown of life, and to be protected from the second death; now He adds two more promises:

> He that hath an ear, let him hear what the Spirit saith to the churches. To him that overcometh, to him I will give of the hidden manna, and I will give him a white stone, and upon the stone a new name written, which no one knoweth it but he that receiveth it.
>
> Verse seventeen

Just as God gave the Jews manna in the wilderness but compromised for food sacrificed to idols, Jesus promises manna to the church in Pergamum. But the church is not to repeat the error. There were many banquets held in Pergamum, and they were held in the temples of the pagan gods. Prior to eating food, it was dedicated to the god of the temple. To those who refused to eat in these banquets, Jesus promised to give the great banquet of eternal life in the kingdom of God. There is some manna in the Ark of the Covenant, which is now in heaven. This is the manna that Jesus promises to the church of Pergamum.

Jesus' second gift is special. It will be a white stone with a new name written on it that is only known to the one who receives it and God. In the day in which this was written, a white stone was used by a judge to vote for a person on trial. A white stone was put into a jar with black stones. The person on trial was to reach into the jar and pull out a stone. If the stone was white, the person was acquitted. If the stone was black, the person was sentenced.

For the Christian, the white stone represents the purity of the redeemed person. White represents the person's righteousness in Jesus Christ. He or she has been declared free of sin. It also refers to the unique new nature of the believer. He or she has been declared a new creature in Christ, and that new person is given a new name to use in heaven. This is that "new name" written down in glory.

The Church in Thyatira

Revelation 2:18–29

As we have discussed before, after the death of Alexander the Great, his kingdom was divided up between four of his generals. One of these, Seleucus I, established the state of Pergamum in 282 BC. At this time, Thyatira became a military post on the eastern border of the Seleucus's kingdom. The name *Thyatira* means "the citadel" or "castle of Thya" and indicates that a settlement that was named Thya already existed there before Seleucus refortified it.

Thyatira frequently changed hands between Pergamene and Syrian rule. This meant that no lasting growth was ever possible like that of the cities of Ephesus and Pergamum during this time of its history.

Thyatira lay in an alluvial plain between the Hermus and Calcius rivers, and it was not built on high ground that provided it with a good base from which to defend its position. Its sole purpose was to act as the first line of defense in front of a hostile advancing army and to hinder their movement while the kingdom's main forces were mustered deeper behind the battlefront.

Thyatira was not worth fighting for, except that it would be employed to hinder an advancing army. The garrison stationed here would, therefore, have been composed of the more guerrilla-like warriors who would be less concerned with winning a war than with throwing the enemy into disarray and hindering its speedy onslaught.

Thyatira fell to the Romans in 190 BC and became the first part of the Pergamene kingdom and then part of the province of Asia. When in 133 BC, Thyatira gave itself wholly into the hands of the Roman Empire, an era of both peace and prosperity was ushered in. Thyatira's military importance began to wane, and the city developed into a prosperous commercial center.

Under Roman control, Thyatira derived its strength and wealth from being in a central place for communications. In the city were numerous types of workers in wool, linen, leather, and bronze; also, potters, tanners, bakers, slavers, and dyers (see Acts 16:14). It was one of the places where dye called "purple" was manufactured. Kings and nobility would come from miles around to purchase it. Purple in the ancient world was a sign of high rank because of the very high cost involved in obtaining the dye.

Most purple dyes were extracted from oysters, but the dye used in Thyatira seems to have been extracted from the roots of certain plants that yielded a bright scarlet end product. The color was extremely rare, and since it came only from Thyatira, the sellers of Thyatira purple were generally very rich traders.

Along with the sellers of purple, there have been more trade guilds identified as existing in Thyatira than any other Asian city of its time. Guilds were officially sanctioned bodies with legal powers and had the right to own property and legislate and initiate public works programs. So, the businessmen received many advantages, both social and economic, from membership in these guilds. Such societies served a useful and sometimes humane faction, but their gatherings were connected with idolatrous worship and often led to immoral conduct.

Membership in a guild was compulsory and refusal to join made it impossible to continue in a trade. They were, as we would say today, closed shops. In the guild's membership, they had regular fellowship meals. Each guild was combined with the worship of a pagan deity, and the members pledged their support to their god and to one another while joining together for a sacrificial meal. Food was first sacrificed to their idol, and the leftovers were served to the guild members. Orgies at these gatherings were a frequent occurrence. It was through participation in these events that those in the guilds came to know each other well, and their commercial and financial security was assured through these contacts.

All of these were anti-Christian, and the church in Thyatira was born in an alien environment. The guilds of the city would have nothing to do with the Christians. There was simply no way to thrive in harmony between these two different ways of life.

Of the pagan deities worshipped in Thyatira, the major god was Apollo Tyrimnos, the Greek sun god. Tyrimnos is depicted as a warrior riding forth to battle, armed with a battle-ax, the symbol of smashing military power. Such a god was natural to a military town such as Tyrimnos. There were other deities such as Artemis, and there were those who followed the pagan religions that sought to introduce evil doctrine into the church.

The streams around Thyatira were filled with leeches, which were collected and exported for wide use in the medicine of the day. One writer says that "In the Thyatiran church, there were human leeches who sucked the spiritual blood out of the church" (Tatford, *The Patmos Letters*, 90). There certainly is truth in that statement!

And now we get to the letter to the church in Thyatira: of all of the seven churches mentioned in the second and third chapters of the book of Revelation, Thyatira would have been considered the least important in the eyes of the world.

Yet, of the seven letters, the one to Thyatira is the longest of all (229 words in Greek compared with 147 to Ephesus, 98 to Smyrna, 147 to Pergamum, 142 to Sardis, 194 to Philadelphia, and finally, 187 to Laodicea).

This doesn't mean that God considered the city to be more important than the other six. All of the seven messages were of equal importance to the specific fellowships that received them. What was important about each of the letters was that they are a dynamic and living word coming from God, via John, to a part of the body of Christ.

Equally important, then, was how the letters were received by the fellowships they were sent to.

Unfortunately, we have no idea, in Thyatira's case, just what their response was, but we need to arm ourselves with the attitude that when God speaks personally to us as a body, we take heed and act on what He says. As God says to all the seven churches, "He that hath an ear, let him hear what the Spirit saith to the churches" (Revelation 2:29).

God holds us accountable to respond adequately to what we know is His voice but not accountable to respond to what we are unsure is His voice.

God speaks plainly; He doesn't mumble. Those who desire to hear God's voice will not miss it, however long He remains silent before speaking.

"To the angel of the church in Thyatira write: These things saith the Son of God, who hath his eyes like a flame of fire, and his feet or unto burnished brass" (verse eighteen).

Forty-nine times the title "Son of God" appears in the New Testament (not counting the term "Son," which stands alone and which by context means "Son of God" at least forty-six times), and we are constantly reminded of the title in numerous hymns and choruses, many sermons, countless conversations with fellow Christians, and arguments with non-Christians (and those who infrequent the news media who take upon themselves the nominal label of "Christian")!

It is not surprising, therefore, if we find nothing unusual in the use of the title, but upon a closer inspection, we discover that it is indeed quite strange to find it both in this particular letter and in this particular book of the New Testament.

This is the only one of the seven letters that contains the title "Son of God" as a title for Jesus. Indeed, it is of even more significance that the introductions to the other six letters are repeats of the description of Jesus already recorded in Revelation 1:12–20 (excluding those to Philadelphia and Laodicea); "Son of God" does not appear there (though "Son of Man" is the title used), nor, for that matter, does it appear anywhere else throughout the entire book of Revelation.

It is, therefore, quite significant that this title is used here. "Son of God" stands in strong contrast to the local cultic worship of Apollo Tyrimnos. This cult was merged with that of the emperor (identified as Apollo Incarnate) so that both were acclaimed as sons of Zeus.

Zeus, the chief god of the Greeks, was the supreme god over all the other pagan gods that existed. Zeus would therefore have taken the place of YHWH in the minds of the Greeks and eventually come to be considered to be the lord over all (we do not for a moment make the assertion that YHWH is Zeus, only that the latter came to be regarded as sovereign in much the same way as YHWH is). Thus, it is not the emperor or the guardian deity of Thyatira but the resurrected Christ who is the true "Son of God."

Apollo was one of the sons of Zeus, the twin of the goddess Artemis (see Acts 19:23–41), by birth to Leto, his mother. Being a "son of Zeus," therefore, meant that he was a son of the supreme Greek god, a "son of god." That the emperor also took upon himself this title is not surprising, as they were regarded as being divine and were worshipped as such throughout the empire.

But the emperor had to be the "son of god" made incarnate who dwelt among mankind.

Thus, the true "Son of God," Jesus, would have been an affront to the state religion and, more specifically, the religion of Thyatira, which worshipped Apollo, the son of god, and the emperor, the incarnate son of god.

By reminding the Thyatirans of His unique divine Sonship, Jesus elevates His own words over and above the authority of anything that would have, as its origin, the cult religion that existed in their city.

Of additional interest here is the prophetic nature of the Apollo cult.

Without going into the reasons for, and the myths beyond this following characteristic, it should be noticed that Apollo's medium or mouthpiece on the earth was the Pythia ("python"), a local woman over fifty years of age who delivered oracles under his (supposed) inspiration. The word is used in Acts 16:16, where the slave girl is said to have a "python" spirit by which she prophesied or (soothsaid). If we are meant to understand that this slave girl was a Pythia, then she would have been a leading figure in the city of Philippi.

If the Pythia passes on words from the deity, then she must remain silent when Apollo speaks directly. Therefore, by speaking as "Son of God," Jesus obviously overrules anything and all that she has already taught and that she might teach in the coming days in contradiction to the content of this letter to the church.

The terms "eyes like a flame" and "feet like burnished bronze" have a particular meaning to the church in Thyatira. The reference of the "feet like bronze" is not recorded in any other book of the Scriptures.

The Greek word for "burnished bronze" is chalcilibanos, which is identified as being a particular type of bronze manufactured in the city of Thyatira; in the first reference to "burnished bronze" in Revelation 1:15, the words "refined [as] in a furnace" are added to the description, which would indicate some sort of commercial processes alluded to.

The description of Jesus here implies that He is the Refiner of His people. The context of this letter also indicates that He is seeking to refine His church from the false teaching and practice (see 1 Corinthians 3:12–15).

Fire (which can also be used to denote God's refining process, which is an integral part of the production of bronze) is used as a description of the wrath of God that burns against sin. Thus, this description of Jesus' feet and eyes is taken particularly to refer equally to these two characteristics of God: as a Purifier of His people and as One who displays His anger toward sin.

God is both angry with His church and seeking to refine her. He is ready to judge but also to extend mercy. His anger will be poured out upon those that follow the heresies of the city, yet, at the same time, the clause "except they repent" (verse twenty-two) adds a note of mercy and forgiveness should the church turn to Him for healing (see also 1 Corinthians 3:12–15).

As in the first half of the verse, there is a significant contrast between how Jesus describes Himself to the Thyatirans and how Apollo was regarded.

Apollo was the god who punished wrongdoers and purified penitents; he was the one "who made men aware of their own guilt and purified them of it" (*Encyclopaedia Britannica Online*, s.v. "Apollo"). Both "feet like burnished bronze" and "eyes like a flame of fire" would be adequate descriptions of Apollo because they speak to us of one who is both angry with men on account of their sin and who seeks to purify them from it.

Again, Jesus reminds the Thyatirans that His position is one of preeminence and superiority over Apollo. Not only does He reveal sin (through the Holy Spirit) in order to forgive, but He is the One who has paid the price for sin through the sacrifice of Himself. Having thus dealt with sin, He is justified in His anger when individuals refuse to accept His work and receive the forgiveness of God by failing to turn to Him in repentance and forsake their ways.

"I know thy works, and thy love and faith and ministry and patience, and that thy last works are more than the first" (verse nineteen).

Jesus, as in most of the other letters, commends the church for what they are doing that is pleasing in His sight, and, in the case of Thyatira, the list is quite impressive. He finds their works—love, service, and patient endurance—worthy of commendation.

However, in spite of this great progression in their walk with Christ, they have a major and potentially suicidal doctrine that is spreading in their midst. It is quite true to say that wherever God's work blossoms, there is the danger of heresy. You can't control its appearance by restricting the church's freedom, but it must be dealt with by strong leadership whenever it shows itself.

As we will see, though the leadership had provided opportunity and encouragement for the body of believers to develop in these areas, they had not been bold enough to oppose the false teaching that had gained both access and adherents within their ranks.

> But I have this against thee, that thou sufferest the woman Jezebel, who calleth herself a prophetess; and she teacheth and seduceth my servants to commit fornication, and to eat things sacrificed to idols.
>
> Verse twenty

The dilemma that faced Christian artisans must have been a simple but extremely difficult one. Coming to Christ meant the loss of their livelihood and financial resources for the church if they abstained from the communal feasts. Participation would be to renounce the faith that they had received and to deny the One who had suffered and died for them. A craftsman continued participation in the trade guild communal feasts was unacceptable to Jesus, but if he were to withdraw from them, he would most likely lose his livelihood and business. The others in the guild would "close him down" by the withdrawal of their support and help. If it was true that a trade guild supported its own and cared for its numbers, it was equally true that any guild was vehemently opposed to competitors who were not part of it. The guild would seek ways to remove them from the competition. Commercial suicide was the result of nonparticipation, but spiritual suicide was the result of a union with their idolatrous practices.

Nevertheless, a woman whom Jesus refers to as Jezebel managed to work out a theology that compromised faith in Christ with continued participation in the trade guilds. This meant continued financial prosperity and material wealth for the Christians. It was believed that this was not the woman's real name but is used to describe her bad teaching. The name "Jezebel" was used to signify that the sin of this individual in the fellowship was like that of her namesake in the Old Testament. It is similar to the use of the name "Balaam" in Revelation 2:14, and it is to her namesake that we must turn in order for us to understand the reason for the Lord's use of the name here.

We first read of Jezebel in 1 Kings 16:31 (ESV), where it is recorded of King Ahab of Israel.

> And as if it had been a light thing for him to walk in the sins of Jeroboam the son of Nebat, he took for his wife Jezebel the daughter of Ethbaal king of the Sidonians, and went and served Baal and worshipped him.

Ahab's marriage alliance with Ethbaal (which means, translated, either "with Baal" or "man of Baal") was forbidden by the Mosaic law (Exodus 34:11–16) but, nevertheless, Ahab entered into it almost certainly because, without an allegiance with Ethbaal, he would not have been able to use the excellent ports of Tyre and Sidon as trade routes for his nation's exports. Though for political expediency, the marriage made sense, it represented the introduction of Baal's worship into the northern Kingdom of Israel.

But more than this, Ahab was a weak-willed king who was pulled and pushed about by his wife, Jezebel. It was she who was, in effect, the driving force behind the throne of Israel; it was she who incited both Ahab and the nation to commit spiritual adultery against YHWH.

Notice, in this respect, some of the statements made about her during Ahab's reign:

It was Jezebel who had cut off the prophets of the Lord, not Ahab. It had been at her command that God's servants had been removed from Israel either by exile or, more likely, by martyrdom (1 Kings 18:4).

It was at Jezebel's table that the prophets of both Baal and Asherah (the female consort of Baal) sat. In other words, Jezebel played host to the leaders of the false god and goddess of her native land, indicating that it was her leadership and not Ahab's that was responsible for the promotion of the idolatrous practices (1 Kings 18:19).

It was Jezebel who disregarded the Mosaic law, the law of Israel, and murdered Naboth to obtain possession of the vineyard for her husband. Ahab certainly sulked, but he hadn't plotted murder. He had stood idly by and let his wife sort out his problem. What a contrast here between the king who should be leading the people into righteousness and the wife who is actively leading the king into greater and greater sin! Jezebel showed herself through this incident to be the dynamic driving force behind the throne (1 Kings 21:5–16).

"There was none who sold himself to do what was evil in the sight of the LORD like Ahab, whom Jezebel his wife incited" (1 Kings 21:25, ESV). Notice here that in the summation of the reign of Ahab, Jezebel is seen as the power behind the throne even though Ahab is culpable for what he allowed himself to be let into.

Summarizing then: Ahab was weak-willed, and Jezebel was a strong-willed leader who got her plans established by manipulating her husband's authority, power, and position. In one final example, see how Elijah tells Ahab what to do (1 Kings 18:41–42) and how he obeys without question even though he's king, yet, when he tells Jezebel all that Elijah has done, the reaction is one of authoritarian control and dominance (1 Kings 19:1–2) that puts down, without mercy, everything and everyone that gets in its way.

Returning to the letter of Thyatira, we can see by some of the phrases employed that this Jezebel has the same trait of authoritarian leadership that her Old Testament namesake portrayed.

In Revelation 2:20, it's recorded that Jezebel "calls herself a prophetess." Rather than allowing the Lord to confirm her ministry within the church, she has elevated herself into a position of authority and has self-proclaimed her function.

"And I gave her time that she should repent; and she willeth if not to repent of her fornication" (verse twenty-one).

Jesus gave Jezebel time to stop teaching immorality in the church, but Revelation 2:21 tells us that she refused to repent; even though an opportunity had been given to change her lifestyle, she had stubbornly refused to do any such thing. She willed herself to refuse to repent! The great sign that Elijah had performed on Mount Carmel had offered an opportunity for the Old Testament Jezebel to acknowledge that God's way was the right way, but she had refused to bow the knee before Him and threatened to murder His servant. Just like with Judas, the opportunity for repentance had passed her by.

"Behold, I cast her into a bed, and them that commit adultery with her into great tribulation, except they repent of her works" (verse twenty-two).

For a strong-willed person to dominate a fellowship, there must also be a weak-willed leadership and congregation. The letter again gives us evidence of this.

Just as Ahab had been responsible for the deeds that Jezebel had incited him to perform, so the Thyatiran individuals were responsible for the deeds that this New Testament Jezebel had incited them to participate in, but the deeds remained characteristically hers.

The real problem, or root cause, of the spiritual adultery in Thyatira was not so much Jezebel as the weak-willed believers who allowed themselves to be led into sin by her and the weak-willed leadership who allowed themselves to be dominated by her.

What, then, was the teaching that Jezebel had brought into the church?

We only have a description of the sins that were a result of Jezebel's teaching immorality and eating food that had been offered first as a sacrifice to idols, but, as we have already seen, Thyatiran trade guilds were numerous and powerful, and it is to these institutions that we should look in order for us to perceive what sort of teaching Jezebel was spreading.

It is interesting to contrast the church in Thyatira with the church in Ephesus: the Ephesian church was weak in love, yet faithful to judge false teachers, while the church in Thyatira grew in love but became too tolerant of false doctrine. There is no room in the church for any kind of compromise.

Like Jezebel, the church members were unwilling to repent. Jesus had given Jezebel time to repent, and now He was giving the church an opportunity to repent. His eyes of fire had searched out their thoughts and motives, and He would make no mistake.

In fact, Jesus threatened to use this assembly as a solemn example to *all of the churches* not to tolerate evil. Jezebel, and her children (or those who followed her), would be sentenced to great affliction (Greek: *thlipsis megalan*). Jezebel's doctrine of evil would bring on a type of sickness or pestilence, which would kill those who did not repent of their sins. Jesus would judge the prophetess and her followers once and for all.

"And I will kill her children with death; and all the churches shall know that I am he that searches the reins and hearts: and I will give unto each one of you according to your works" (verse twenty-three).

Not everyone in the church was unfaithful to Jesus. To those who were faithful, He gives an encouraging statement: He has no special demands to make, only that they stand firm in their belief in Him and resist the evil of compromise. He will reward those who are faithful to Him, and His reward will be in comparison to their faithfulness to Him and what they had done in His name.

"But to you I say, to the rest that are in Thyatira, as many as have not this teaching, who know not the deep things of Satan, as they are wont to say; I cast upon you none other burden" (verse twenty-four).

These faithful believers will have no other weight upon them. As long as they remain faithful to Jesus, He will remain faithful to them and give them no burden to bear, for they have not indulged in the worship of satanic idols.

"Nevertheless that which ye have, hold fast till I come" (verse twenty-five).

"Holding fast" just means to continue to resist the evil, which was all around them, and remain true to His Word until He returns for His bride, the church universal. This reference to Jesus' return for His church is the first mention of His coming for the church in the event that we call "the rapture."

The exhortation is to remain faithful to all that they have received from the Lord up to that point. Even though they have progressed in the Christian life in the sense that the quality of their love, faith, service, and endurance has improved, Jesus now lays upon them nothing more than they live up to all that they have already attained.

"And he that overcometh, and he that keepeth my works unto the end, to him will I give authority over the nations" (verse twenty-six).

Those who are able to remain faithful to Jesus will be rewarded when He comes back at the second coming and sets up His millennial kingdom. At that time, He promises those who remained faithful that they will be given authority over the nations that make it through the Tribulation period. The church will rule and reign with Him (see Revelation 20:4).

"And he shall rule them with a rod of iron, as the vessels of the potter are broken to shivers; as I also have received of my Father" (verse twenty-seven).

During the millennial kingdom, Jesus will rule with a powerful hand (with a rod of iron); rebellious men will be like clay pots, easily broken to pieces! Those who are Christians will live in a sin-free society for 1,000 years. During these 1,000 years, Jesus will sit upon the throne of Israel and will rule firmly, righteously, and with perfect justice.

"[...] and I will give him the morning star" (verse twenty-eight).

This further reward promised to the overcomers is described as "the morning star." We will find in the concluding chapter of this book (Revelation 22:16) that Jesus describes Himself as "the bright and morning star." In the prophecy of Numbers 24:17 (KJV), Balaam predicted that "there shall come a star out of Jacob." Centuries later, Peter described in his second letter that the prophetic word would be a light shining in a dark place "until the day dawn, and the day star arise in your hearts" (2 Peter 1:19, KJV).

This refers to the dawn of Jesus' second coming and the ushering in of the millennium kingdom. This pledge to the overcomers in the church in Thyatira is their participation in that day of joy and gladness. The overcomer had the assurance of association with Jesus on that glorious day.

Another implication in this promise directly reflects on the Roman devotees of astrology. The emperors of Rome had become fanatical followers of astrologers. They came to these astrologers with all of their questions concerning the future. Before too long, neither the important nor trivial matters were undertaken without first consulting the "stargazers." They were consulted before going to war, founding a city, marriage, or a change of residence.

So, it is with scarcely veiled irony that Jesus says simply, "I will give you the morning star." Those Christians who were faithful to the Lord saw the star as a promise of revival, reawakening, and resurrection.

The Church in Sardis

Revelation 3:1–6

The city of Sardis was thirty miles southwest of Thyatira. The city was situated on an almost inaccessible plateau about the midpoint of the Hermus River valley. It commanded a position overlooking a junction of the five roads that connected the royal trade routes. At this junction, the roads had to cross the river at a ford across the Hermes River.

A small stream named the Pactolus flowed down from Mount Tmolus and into the Hermus River. This small stream was gold-bearing and was the source of much of Sardis's wealth. Early on, electrum was discovered, and the gold rush was on. Electrum is a mixture of gold and silver. They used the method of anchoring a sheepskin under the water and then shoveling dirt into the stream. As the dirt washed downstream, it flowed over the sheepskins. The lanolin in the sheepskins had the properties to trap the gold and allow the other types of soil to wash on downstream. This was their easy, practical means of extracting the proper ores for refining.

The production of jewelry in both gold and silver reached a very high degree of skill in Sardis. All of the metal techniques known from ancient times were used in Sardis. They used the lost-wax process, which is still used today.

Sardis was the earliest city in the world to use coins as a means of trade and barter, and they cast their coins and stamped them with the seals of the king. When they did the smelting, they used a small crucible, which held only a small amount of the processed metal. Since the amounts smelted were nearly all of the same size, the value is considered to be the same for each ingot. The gold ingots were flattened into a round shape and then were stamped with the likeness of the emperor. They called these discs "coins." The stamped coins were identified by the likeness of the emperor, and thus the resultant coins were known to come from Sardis. As the coins multiplied, they were used as payment for goods. The idea traveled around the world, and economics changed everywhere. This production of coins became the greatest export item of the Lydian empire.

Along with silver and gold, several other ores were mined near Sardis. Cinnabar was found nearby, and this source of mercury was used to silver mirrors. Sulfur was discovered and was used to treat wool before dying and cure camels of the mange.

Sardis was also known for its wool industries and the marble quarried from the Tmolus mountain. Opulence and luxury were the order of the day, and life was good in Sardis.

The city stood just in front of Mount Tmolus. The city site was about 800 feet in altitude above the valley floor, and in order to approach it, you had to climb a steep incline. The city proper was surrounded by three walls, one inside the next, circling the city on three sides. The fourth side of the city backed onto a sheer cliff that was considered to be unscalable. With all of these fortifications, Sardis felt itself to be impregnable. As an example, when Alexander the Great passed through the area on his quest into the interior of Asia Minor, he took notice of the city's strong fortifications and its strategic location and decided not to expend the energy to defeat it in battle and instead bypassed Sardis.

EXAMPLES OF COINS OF ASIA MINOR

LEFT...SILVER TETRADRACHM COIN SHOWING ALEXANDER THE GREAT/FACE, ATHENA AND NIKE/REVERSE. 306-281 B.C. MINTED IN EPHESUS BY: KING LYSIMACHUS OF THRACE. NIKE IS CROWNING LYSMACHUS' NAME WITH A LAUREL WREATH, SYMBOLIZING HIM BEING CROWNED KING.

RIGHT...ELECTRUM COIN/STATER FROM EPHESUS, 625–600 BC. OBVERSE: STAG GRAZING RIGHT, IS ASSOCIATED WITH ARTEMIS. REVERSE POSSIBLY STATES "I AM THE BADGE/SIGN/TOMB OF PHANES/LIGHT"

LEFT...SILVER COIN MINTED IN PERGAMON MID 5TH CENTURY BC. HEAD OF APOLLO WITH LAUREL WREATH RIGHT; MARKING BEHIND NECK / BEARDED HEAD RIGHT. POSSIBLY THE GREEK RULER GONGYLOS.

RIGHT...A COIN OF SMYRNA, TETRADRACHM. TURRETED HEAD OF CYBELE ON THE FACE. REVERSE ΣMYP/NAIR?N WITH A MONOGRAM IN THE CENTER OF AN OAK WREATH. 4TH CENTURY BC.

LEFT...AN ELECTRUM COIN OF ORONTES, ACHAEMENID SATRAP (A GOVERNOR OF A PROVINCE IN THE ANCIENT PERSIAN EMPIRE OF MYSIA WHICH INCLUDED PERGAMON). REVERSE SHOWS PEGASUS. CIRCA 357-352 BC

CARANBURROWSLEAHY

Since the city was considered to be impregnable, the inhabitants totally ignored anyone who attempted to overcome them. Their reputation was such that they didn't even post guards at night, and they depended on their reputation for their defense.

As in most cities in Asia Minor, Caesar's or emperor worship flourished, and like Ephesus, Sardis also housed a large temple devoted to Artemis. The temple stood south of the Royal Road, south of Sardis proper, along the Pactolus River, in the foothills of the Tmolus mountain range. The temple was 160 × 200 feet in size and was one of the largest temples in the Greek world. The construction of this temple took so long that the design was changed every time a new conqueror took over the region. The temple was used in both Greek and Roman times as a treasury, rich enough to lend money to back trade ventures and caravans.

There was also a temple to Cybele, the nature goddess.

As far as the church of Sardis was concerned, the believers had adopted the mindset of the rest of the citizens. They ignored the danger of infiltration and spiritually "went to sleep." The church had become so complacent about their ministry that they ceased to be aggressive. There was no persecution of the church because the unsaved in Sardis saw the church as a respectable group of people who were neither dangerous to them nor desirable for them to join. They were decent people but with a dead witness and a decaying ministry.

And now to the text! It was this negligent attitude that caused Jesus to say to them: "I know thy works, that thou hast a name that thou livest, and thou art dead" (verse one). Jesus focused on the woeful lack of spirituality in the church, not only in the membership but also in the leadership. Through Jesus Christ and the Holy Spirit, all of the ingredients for a dynamic, vibrant church are always available to its people and its leaders. Where there is a lack of spiritual power and life in the church, there is a lack of union with the Lord Jesus Christ. Where there is a lack of union with Him, there is only a form of Christianity.

Jesus is telling them here, "There is no excuse for your pitiful state, so I am sending you this letter in hopes that you will listen and recover." Please note: in every other letter to these churches, Jesus says, "I know your deeds." But here, the deeds are dead! Only one other of the seven churches had nothing good to be said about it, and that was the church in Laodicea, which we will get to soon.

To its shame, the church in Sardis stood as a double contradiction: first, it was not what God intended it to be, and second, it was not what God designed it to be. God intended the church to be alive. It is made up of "living stones"; in it, the Spirit of the living God dwells. Its source of life is Jesus Christ. Whatever the Sardis church was doing, it was not focused on God or His objectives. They didn't desire God's approval; they didn't seek holiness; they didn't have a servant's attitude; they weren't proclaiming the Gospel; they weren't discipling other believers; they weren't evangelizing; they weren't praying regularly as a body of believers; they weren't growing, either in member numbers or spiritually; and they were compromising what little conviction they had. In other words, the church in Sardis was dead! It promised much but delivered nothing.

There are many churches today that once had very good reputations. They preached the gospel of Jesus Christ, but their messages drifted into oblivion. The life of the church is gone, and the doors should have been closed. Today those churches are still open, and some have large congregations, but they are empty shells, for spiritual death came to those assemblies a long time ago.

It is easy for a church to lose it all, and our Lord must grieve as He looks down on so many churches that are not only shells but are totally dead. This is tragic, and believers should not remain in such a church. But getting people to leave their church is like pulling teeth. For the most part, people who have sat in congregations without being spiritually fed have lost their hearing.

However, it is even sadder when our personal Christian lives become like flowers left in a grave, wilted and withered and good only to throw away, and we no longer have a vibrant, spiritual walk with the Lord.

"Be thou watchful, and establish the things that remain, which were ready to die: for I have found no works of thine perfected before my God" (verse two).

In verse two, we have to go back to the history of Sardis to begin to understand what Jesus is saying: in its history, Sardis simply ignored any danger to its well-being. They had been bypassed by the greatest general in all of history, and they felt it was because their city could not be taken. Although Alexander did not bother with Sardis, others did. Cyrus, the king of Persia, had come to Sardis during his battles and had attacked the fortress city. It could be said that he fought an uphill battle all the way, but he could not penetrate its defenses. If his soldiers reached the outer walls, the soldiers within rolled down rocks from the walls, rained arrows down on them, or poured boiling oil on them. Because of the steep slopes, the footing was not very good, so any little impediment to them became serious and stopped them in their tracks. So, the mighty army of Cyrus camped on the plain below the city and tried to figure out how they could overcome Sardis.

Cyrus offered a reward to anyone who could come up with a plan to penetrate the defenses of the city. One afternoon, one of Cyrus's officers was reconnoitering and observed a Sardinian soldier atop the cliff in the back of the city, going to the bathroom. The soldier dropped his helmet, and the helmet tumbled down the cliff. The officer was amazed to see the soldier nonchalantly descend the cliff by way of a winding path that could not be seen from below, retrieve his helmet, and climb back up to the city. The officer made a mental note of the route to the city the soldier had taken and reported back to Cyrus.

The inhabitants of the city had totally ignored guarding the cliff as a means of attack because of its steepness. They didn't even post guards there at night. The reputation of impregnability lulled them, literally, to sleep. The entire army went to bed, and while they were asleep, Cyrus's army climbed the cliff by way of the path the officer had observed, and his army went through the city and killed all of the defending soldiers.

They had depended on their reputation rather than their actions! With one of the most powerful armies ever mustered in the world, they ignored the danger and went to sleep. They had "a name." But their "name" couldn't save them. The next day they were all dead. They had not paid attention to their vulnerable spots and hadn't posted their guards, and because of this, they perished.

When Jesus used these terms to the church in Sardis, they should have gotten the point, but they didn't! The church would have been better off had there been some kind of suffering, but it had grown comfortable and complacent and was living on its reputation. The problem was that the reputation wasn't theirs but that of their predecessors. Like the city of Sardis, the church gloried in its past splendor but ignored its present decay.

There are many churches today that are dead spiritually. They, too, are like the church in Sardis. They are trying to live on their past reputation. And like the church in Sardis, present-day churches will die. Why? Because they have become accustomed to their blessings, and they have become complacent about their ministry, and have gone to bed and slept while the enemy found a way in.

Jesus said to them, "Wake up! The enemy has come into your church, and you aren't even aware of it. You are sound asleep spiritually. Your centurions are asleep." No one was guarding their fortress, the church of Jesus Christ. No one can ever say that the church of Sardis wasn't given fair warning. Remember therefore how thou hast received and didst hear; and keep it, and repent. If therefore thou shalt not watch, I will come as a thief, and thou shalt not know what hour I will come upon thee.

Verse three

To the church in Sardis, Jesus said, "Be alert, go back to the way your church was originally." Those at the church in the past

87

had heard the Gospel message and had responded. They had received salvation, but that was not the case in the present assembly. They had become complacent and had not really repented. "Or else," Jesus said, "there will be sudden destruction. I will do to you what Cyrus did to the city back in 549 BC. Come out of your stupor!"

They were to go back to the fundamental doctrines of the faith and repent of their spiritual emptiness. Failure to comply would bring judgment from the Lord, who would come upon them as a thief. And here in Revelation, chapter three, Jesus is using the same terminology of the thief as He used in 1 Thessalonians 5:2–3:

> For yourselves know perfectly that the day of the Lord so cometh as a thief in the night. When they are saying, Peace and safety, then sudden destruction cometh upon them, as travail upon a woman with child; and they shall in no wise escape.

In the history of the church, the Lord often removes a spiritually dead congregation rather than let it continue to infect others with its decadence. My wife, Ann, and I were in London many years ago and visited the largest church building ever constructed in England. It is no longer a church but only a museum. In Munich, we saw a church that was only used as a tourist trap that had guides who would take you on a tour of the building for a fee. Both of these were beautiful, dead buildings. Their congregations are long dead and gone. They had all been closed by Jesus Christ!

"But thou hast a few names in Sardis that did not defile their garments: and they shall walk with me in white; for they are worthy" (verse four).

Once again, Jesus uses terminology that is not familiar to the casual reader of this book. The pagan religions of Sardis forbade their followers to come before their gods with clothing that was stained or soiled. Those who did so were removed from the public ledger as citizens of Sardis. Christians who soiled their garments were seen as mingling with the pagan life of the city and compromising with sin. Jesus says that those who did not defile their garments would be walking with Him in white, for their faithfulness had kept them spiritually clean. There were a few in the church who weren't living sinful lives. They had not given in to spiritual death.

"He that overcometh shall thus be arrayed in white garments; and I will in no wise blot his name out of the book of life, and I will confess his name before my Father, and before his angels" (verse five).

White raiment is symbolic of purity and righteousness and is the symbol of salvation. In this letter, it is symbolic of the faithful remnant who would gain spiritual victory over the paganism of Sardis. We see that at the marriage of the Lamb, Revelation 19:7–8, all believers will be arrayed in fine white linen and will return to the earth with Jesus clothed in those garments.

And the name of the overcomer will remain in the book of life; that is, the overcomer's name is recorded in the divine register of those who belong to Jesus. This corresponds to another of the practices in Sardis, where the names of individuals were recorded in the city register. After their death or departure from the populace of the city, their names were erased from or marked out of the book of the living. This is an affirmation that those who are born again have eternal life and that no person or thing can ever separate Christians from eternal life. It is better to be an overcomer than an undertaker.

And then, Jesus will declare the believer's name to God the Father. This promises the believer the assurance of eternal citizenship. Jesus is our advocate before God the Father and will acknowledge each Christian's name to God. This will occur during the seven years that the church will be in heaven, while the seven years of tribulation are occurring on the earth. In addition, Jesus will introduce each Christian to the heavenly beings.

"He that hath an ear, let him hear what the Spirit saith to the churches" (verse six).

Jesus concludes His letter to the church in Sardis with the same words used to the other churches in Asia Minor. Sardis is to be aware: they have been warned! They need to heed the words written in this letter and turn their lives around. This warning is significant to a spiritually dead church like Sardis. And if we are honest, our church needs to heed this message as well. For if we were to take our spiritual temperature, would it be a fever level, just so-so, or not even so-so? Are we dead or alive in Christ?

We need to tune our ears to God's Word now.

Chapter Three

The Church in Philadelphia

Philadelphia was located in the Hermus River valley, about thirty miles southeast of Sardis. The city was founded in 140 BC by Attalus II, the king of Pergamum. He had a brother of whom he was very fond and whose name was Eumenes, whom he succeeded. The name *Philadelphia* comes from the Greek word *philadelphus*. The name means "brotherly love" in the Greek language and describes the loyalty and affection between the two brothers. Coins from Philadelphia show the two brothers as completely alike in height, features, and dress.

The city was built twenty-five miles from the junction of the Hermus and Cogamus rivers at the upper end of the valley, which climbed into the mountains behind it. It was built on a volcanic mountain range some 900 feet high and experienced many earthquakes. When the city was destroyed by an earthquake in AD 17, it was rebuilt by Emperor Tiberius. The city prospered due to its location and rich, fertile valley. Along with its grape industry (wines), Philadelphia was also noted for its textiles and leather goods.

Because of its high position at the point where the Piedmont region ended and the mountains began, Philadelphia became the imperial post of the Roman Empire and was known to the world as the "Gateway to the East." At the site of the city, there was a long cleft in the otherwise sheer cliffs, which was the only entrance into the central plane of Asia Minor for hundreds of miles.

Philadelphia was built on the great trade route, which ran through Pergamum and Sardis before going into Asia Minor. If trouble came, the gates of Philadelphia would be closed and locked, and its fortifications would withstand a great deal of force against it. Since it was the only route into western Asia Minor, it became a very important city.

The primary religious practice in Philadelphia was the worship of Janus, also known as Tammuz, the Babylonian two-headed god. Janus, if you remember, was the son of Nimrod and Semiramis. After Nimrod died, Semiramis gave birth to Janus, whom she announced was Nimrod reborn. The worship of Janus was an offshoot of the mother-goddess worship of Semiramis, or Cybele, as she was known in this region.

Janus was known as a mediator between the earth and heaven and, according to pagan ideas, had all of the power in heaven, on the earth, and the seas. In this position, he was said to have the power of turning "the hinge" (Alexander Hislop, *The Two Babylons*): of opening the doors of heaven or shutting the gates of peace or war upon the earth. Janus was also known as "Dionysus," the god of wine. In view of the large production of wine in the Cogamus valley and the quantities sold in the markets of Philadelphia, this is not surprising. The worship of Dio-

nysus attracted many people with its freedom, revelry, danc-
ing, and sensual enjoyment.

By its position, immediately after Sardis, Philadelphia
seems to represent the last effort of the Holy Spirit together
with all of the living children of the family of God. Most commentators on the letter to the church of Philadelphia write that
nothing in the church merited reprimand or criticism. But
those who write thusly have not studied the relationship between this church and the religions practiced in Philadelphia.

In Jesus' opening statement, he dictates,

> And to the angel of the church in Philadelphia write:
> These things saith he that is holy, he that is true, he
> that hath the key of David, he that openeth and none
> shall shut, and that shutteth and none openeth: I
> know thy works (behold, I have set before thee a door
> opened, which none can shut).
>
> Verses seven to eight

These words are directed to counter the false teaching of the
pagan religion that defied Janus. Janus did not have the power
to open or close the doors of heaven and earth. Nor was he able
to control peace and war. Jesus is the only One who has such
power.

In ancient history, Janus is always depicted as having two
heads. His mother claimed that he was "twice-born." This is to
say the Janus was also Nimrod reborn. Thus, Janus was Semiramis's husband and son. This is shown in almost every pagan religion that has a mother goddess. These religions have twisted

the account of Noah and the ark and show Noah as being "buried" in the ark for over a year and then being reborn. Therefore, the ark of Noah was not a boat but a coffin. The connection comes from the religion practiced in Egypt, which replaces Noah with Osiris. In this religion, the ship of Isis and the coffin of Osiris are the same as Noah and the ark. This is the central theme in the festival known as "the Disappearance of Osiris." At the end of the year, Osiris is said to have been "twice-born," or "regenerated."

There is much more to say about Janus, but His letter is not about Janus but the church. We will go back to the keys of Janus as opposed to the keys of Jesus: first, in the pagan religion that was practiced in Philadelphia, there were two keys. They were the keys to heaven and earth. In this religion, Janus was given a key, and Cybele was given a key. Two keys were the symbol of power. Remember, Cybele here is just another name for Semiramis. Now comes the point that I would rather not mention, but in dividing the Word of God, I must. In the early church and in Philadelphia, there was a movement to bring in a priesthood. Jesus had already spoken about the Nicolaitans in the previous letters and said He hated the doctrine and their teaching. But the same thing was happening again.

Janus was known as the God of doors and hinges and was called the opener and shutter. Of note is the Greek word for a hinge. It is *cardo*. The term "cardinal" is derived from cardo. The Roman Catholic pope's grand council of state is known even today as the College of Cardinals. The pope is said to have possession of Janus's keys and, therefore, has inherited the duties and power of Janus. Whatever important business was at hand, whenever deity was to be invoked, an invocation must have first been addressed to Janus, who was recognized as the god of gods.

It was the same religious teaching that prevailed when Jesus sent a letter to the church, rebuking the profane ascription of His position and dignity and asserting His claim to the powers usually attributed to Janus.

To this Janus worshipped in Asia Minor, and equally in early times in Rome, belonged all power in heaven, on the earth, and in the sea, according to pagan religions. In this character, he was said to have the "power of turning the hinge." The Roman Catholic pope is set up in the same position as Janus and also has the power of turning the hinge.

In the countries where the Babylonian religious systems are practiced today, we find the leaders of the religions with the very same attributes ascribed to Janus.

"Thou hast a little power, and didst keep my word, and did not deny my name" (verse eight, part b).

You would think, by reading this verse, that the church of Philadelphia had some power left, but in Greek, it reads, "Thou hast little power." That's like saying, "My chances are little to none." Almost like saying that they were too weak to get out of bed. They were too feeble to do anything. Yet, the church had not completely rejected Jesus.

> Behold, I give [you] of the synagogue of Satan, of them that say they are Jews, and they are not, but do lie; behold, I will make them to come and worship before thy feet, and to know that I have loved thee.
>
> Verse nine

Like some of the other churches in Asia Minor, the church of Philadelphia suffered at the hands of a large number of unbelieving Jews in the city. They constantly tried to bring the Jewish worship practices into the church. Jesus refers to these as the "Synagogue of Satan." Not only were they trying to infiltrate the church but also attempting to bring the priesthood into the worship system. The time that Jesus is referring to is when the Jews here would fall down at the feet of the Christians at Philadelphia is still future. When He returns to rule the earth, every single Jew who fomented a change to the pure worship of Jesus at Philadelphia will be forced to kneel before the congregation and acknowledge that they were wrong about the church and the Christians there.

"Because thou didst keep the word of my patience, I will also keep thee from the hour of trial, that hour which is to come upon the whole world, to try them that dwell upon the earth" (verse ten).

This verse is one of the most comforting verses in future prophecy for the people of the Christian church. If we look ahead to the remaining chapters of the Revelation, the plagues, war, and the destruction that will come have had Christians concerned for generations. God's children were wondering if they survived. Fortunately, God has made promises for His people concerning the Great Tribulation. First, look at the verse! If Christians are faithful, God says that He will do something for us. What does the verse say? "I will keep thee from the hour of trial."

Jesus also says that this hour of trial is to come "upon the whole world." Then He adds, "to try them that dwell upon the earth." If Christians are kept "from the hour," it would mean that we would still be here when this happens because we would be dwelling on the earth. So, what happens to us? The English language would seem to infer that we will still be here during the Tribulation period. However, a close examination of this verse in Greek shows us that the English translation is incorrect. In Greek, Jesus said that He will keep us "out of" the hour of trial.

The Greek word for "from" is *apo*. The word used in this verse is ek. While both are adjectives, *apo*, when translated into English, is "from"; the word *ek* used here is translated into English is "out of." So, simply said, when the Tribulation period comes upon the earth and its inhabitants, the Christians will be gone "out of" the earth's sphere!

Combined with other scripture verses, this is one of the most definite proof texts for the rapture of the church prior to the beginning of the Tribulation. God's wrath will be poured out on the earth. Romans 5:9 says, "Much more then, being now justified by his blood, shall we be saved from the wrath of God through him." Again, ek is used in Greek: not "from" but "out of." If God's wrath is poured out upon all who dwell on the earth and we are guaranteed no wrath, then it stands to reason that Christians will be gone from the earth!

"I come quickly: hold fast that which thou hast, then no one take thy crown" (verse eleven).

Again, in Greek, Jesus is saying, "When I come, I will come swiftly." When Jesus comes for the church, His arrival will not be announced. The Christians which He is coming for must be ready to go. Make sure that you were really saved. When Jesus comes for the church, if you are not saved, you will not receive the "crown of life," which is eternal life.

> He that overcometh, I will make him a pillar in the temple of my God, and he shall go out thence no more: and I will write upon him the name of my God, and the name of the city of my God, the new Jerusalem, which cometh down out of heaven from my God, and mine own new name.
>
> verse twelve

In the church, there are pillars and caterpillars. A pillar holds up the church, and a caterpillar just crawls in and out. This strength is in comparison to the little strength that they had presently. It was a common practice in Philadelphia for a pagan religion to erect a pillar in their temple inscribed with the name of a person to note the details of the actions of that person. I will compare this with those churches that put nameplates on the windows, doors, and pews of churches when a person pays for them.

In the pagan religions of Philadelphia, a person had the name of the city on his forehead and was declared free. A Christian's citizenship was inactive, and they did not have the name of the city displayed. It was also common for the priests of pagan idolatry to have the name of their God written on their forehead. So, the overcomer will be one of the strong supporters in the temple of God and will have God's name, God's city name, and Jesus' new name written on him or her and would be marked as belonging to Him. We will also see more about Jesus' new name later in Revelation 19:12.

"He that hath an ear, let him hear with the Spirit saith to the churches" (verse thirteen).

And once more, we hear this same message: open your spiritual ears and make this message meaningful in your own life. This letter is written to you also. Listen up. And learn!

The Church in Laodicea

Revelation 3:14–22

In the circle of churches, we have come to the last of the seven. The city of Laodicea is south of Philadelphia and directly east of Ephesus. Laodicea was founded by Antiochus II as a Seleucid city. The city was named *Laodicea* after Antiochus's wife, Laodicea. The name means "justice of the people" and comes from two Greek words, *laos* and *dikaios*. Laos means "people," and dikaios means "to do one justice."

The city was strategically well placed. It was located at the junction of three much-traveled highways and grew in a highly successful commercial center. It was a city of wealthy bankers and financiers, and its theaters, huge stadium, lavish public baths, and fabulous shopping centers gave ample evidence of the luxury enjoyed by its inhabitants.

One of the principal highways of Asia Minor ran through this city, and it should have been an important military center because it stood on the way into the interior province of Phrygia. However, it was not adequate as the fortress city. It had one major weakness, which robbed Laodicea of all military use! The city did not have an adequate water supply with which to support a long siege from an oppressing army.

The nearest water source was from the Lycus River, which was about two miles outside the city, and this water was not fit to drink. If they were attacked by an invading army, their source of water could easily be cut off.

Their water supply came from the nearby cities of Colossae and Hierapolis, two other cities that formed a triangle with Laodicea. The water was transported to Laodicea by way of aqueducts. These aqueducts were formed from three-foot-wide hollowed-out stone blocks, which were laid in an overhead aqueduct system.

The water of the area was sulfurous. The water piped in from Hierapolis was hot, and the water piped in from Colossae was cold, and since the distance the water flowed was about six miles, by the time the water arrived in Laodicea, it was lukewarm. This will be of significance when we deal with verses fifteen and sixteen.

If an invading army cut off the water supply, Laodicea would be helpless, and this weakness ruined the character of the city as a strong fortress and must have prevented people there from ever feeling secure when threatened.

Since the city was more or less militarily defenseless, it had become a commercial and financial center. It maintained peace through its wishy-washy, noncommittal way of approaching the different people who passed through.

The city became a center of banking and financial institutions; it was a place where money changing was a common practice. The city minted its own coins from gold brought down from the interior and refined it in Laodicea. The bankers boasted of the city's riches and their ability to meet all demands made upon them.

In AD 17 and AD 61, earthquakes destroyed the city, and when offered relief from the Roman Senate, it refused and effected a complete recovery unaided. The citizens prided themselves on their self-sufficiency and independent spirit. By their own exertions, Laodicea became one of the most flourishing cities in Asia Minor.

Its prosperity was due largely to its location. Caravans from all points of the compass passed through Laodicea. Its trade was conducted with countries from all over the world. Much wealth flowed through the city, and much stayed there.

From the beginning, Laodicea was a success story. The Laodiceans had a breed of sheep raised in that district that was different from any other in the world. The wool of the sheep was black, and its glossy raven-colored beauty was superior to any other to be found in the world. They produced a valuable sort of wool cloth, soft in texture and glossy black in color. This wool was coveted around the world and was woven into garments of several kinds and used at home and exported. They made a number of types of garments, and one type of tunic, called trimita was so famous that the city was listed in some documents as Trimitaria. This breed of sheep has now completely disappeared.

All in all, Laodicea was an affluent society with little interest in anything but the material. As a military city, it had its defects, but its status as a center of commerce was not to be despised. It was a proud and self-satisfied city, well aware of its economic status.

The wealthy city might have been expected to produce a flourishing and spiritually powerful church, but the character of the city had affected the Christians too. Jesus' description of the church portrays a wishy-washy body whose principal interest was in material prosperity rather than the spiritual good.

Outside the city was a famous temple to the Phyrigian god Men Karou. This was the original pagan god of the valley. The temple was the center of society, administration, trade, and religion. All religions were governed so that they proceeded in an orderly manner. A market was held under the protection of this "god," and the people of the valley met and traded with strangers who came for their products.

In connection with the temple was a famous school of medicine. This school was another of the same kind as the school in Pergamum. They worshipped the snake god, and the coins they minted in the temple had the serpent-encircled staff of Asclepius stamped into the metal.

Their god, Men Karou, is said to be the king and father of his people, and even when the Hellenic civilization took over the area, the people continued to worship their old native god. This god was sometimes called Aseia, which means "powerful," and was known to come to the area from Syria.

The Laodicean school of physicians followed the techniques of Herophilos, who, on the principle that compound diseases require compound medicines, began to mix medicines, which carried down to our century and were used until they were finally removed from our list of pharmaceuticals.

There was an ointment for treating ears made from the spice nard, also known as spikenard. This was originally prepared only in Laodicea, but after the second century, it was made in other cities.

Eyesalve was also discovered in Laodicea, made from Phrygian stone and ground into a powder. "Phrygian" was often used in place of Laodicean, and Phrygian stone was exported into all parts of the Greek and Roman empires and, when mixed with oil, was used by physicians to treat eye ailments. This salve is still used around the world.

In AD 62, a Roman governor prohibited the export of gold. They were running out of gold, and they needed to keep it in order to bolster their currency. Once a year, every male Jew above twenty-one years of age sent half a shekel to the temple in Jerusalem to support the worship of Jehovah there. When they tried to ship their offerings to Jerusalem, the Roman governor promptly confiscated them. Their shipment weighed twenty pounds. In today's money, that would be $136,480.00 that the Roman governor stole from God.

"And to the angel of the church in Laodicea write: These things saith the Amen, the faithful and true witness, the beginning of the creation of God" (verse fourteen).

Jesus deemed the church in Laodicea was unstable and unreliable, and He presented Himself to it in a threefold character, which was extremely appropriate to its condition. Once again, He addresses a letter to the "angel," or the pastor of the church. This letter was to be read to the entire congregation.

He identifies Himself as the "Amen," which literally means "so be it!" Another way to phrase this: Jesus is calling Himself the final word. We use the term in church to put the final exclamation mark on our messages or prayers to God, and here Jesus is putting His final exclamation to the church in Laodicea in this message. His second identification is "the faithful witness." Many others have borne witness for God, but there has been only One whose testimony was marked by undeviating fidelity and unswerving loyalty. He faithfully represented the Father and bore witness to Him, even in the face of death, and if all other testimony for God has been defective, Jesus has never wavered.

Jesus also refers to Himself as Creator, the active Source and Author of creation. In John 1:3 (NKJV), John writes, "All things were made by Him, and without Him was nothing made that was made." Jesus is the preeminent One. He is supreme, above the creation.

"I know thy works, that thou art neither cold nor hot: I would thou wert cold or hot" (verse fifteen).

The Laodicean church was neither cold nor hot but lukewarm. It was vastly indifferent. It was indifferent to doctrine, to truth, and to the teaching of God and the great fundamental truths that God reveals in His book. The Laodicean church was not only lukewarm and indifferent about the great truth and doctrine of God, but its members did not even know the truth and the doctrine of God. What did the church believe?

What did it stand for? What was its teaching? What were its goals? They didn't know, and they didn't care! If they had either been hot or cold, then they could have been ministered to, but in their wishy-washy state, they refused to listen to anyone.

"So because thou art lukewarm, and neither hot nor cold, I will spew thee out of my mouth" (verse sixteen).

The people in the church in Laodicea knew what Jesus was saying because He used the local water situation to describe their spiritual condition. They had lived with lukewarm sulfur water all their lives. They knew that sulfur water was good tasting if it was hot or cold, but lukewarm, it was nauseating.

Their indifference to Him and the Word of God was just as nauseating. What created this condition? There is only one answer—compromise! When you want to make something lukewarm, you mix hot and cold together. Then what you get is neither. The church in Laodicea was mixing spirituality with paganism. It was more comfortable for them to be wishy-washy than to make a stand for Jesus. They were compromising their basic teachings for the sake of peace with their pagan neighbors. It was a comfortable church. It required nothing from its members, and consequently, it got nothing from them. They were never challenged, rebuked, corrected, or exhorted. They had become like a religious country club. The people may have liked their church, but Jesus didn't, and He told them very literally that they made Him want to puke!

There can be no real Christianity without enthusiasm. Jesus loves the man who throws himself with abandon into the spiritual arena. He likes enthusiasm, like the man who smashed through his neighbors' roof to get his friend closer to Jesus to be healed, or Zacchaeus, who abandoned his dignity and climbed up the sycamore tree. He praised the woman who pestered the idle judge until he gave her justice. But those of the church in Laodicea just made Him want to throw up!

"Because thou sayest, I am rich, and have gotten riches, and have need of nothing; and knowest not that thou art the wretched one and miserable and poor and blind and naked" (verse seventeen).

The church in Laodicea was fat, dumb, and happy. It was smug; it was self-sufficient, and it was complacent. They had plenty of money, probably a nice building in which to meet, and they had the respect of the surrounding community. They thought they were doing well, but Jesus takes one look and tells it like it is!

Jesus was using one measurement for the church, but they were using another. It was as if they were using centigrade and Jesus was using Fahrenheit. Laodicea was using the standards of the world. Their standards were comfortable, approved by the surrounding community, and they thought they were in good shape. But the church is not to be run for the benefit of its members! It is not a country club; it is not a political action club, and it is not a performing arts center.

Jesus tells us plainly what His church is to be like. It is to be salt! And not just plain salt, but salty salt. He says in the Gospel accounts, "Salt that loses its saltiness is good for nothing" (Matthew 5:13; Mark 9:50; Luke 14:34, paraphrased). Salt without saltiness is to be thrown out and walked on. But a church should be salty. Like salt in food, it should be spread throughout the whole area, flavoring whatever it touches. The church should function every day of the week, not just on Sunday.

The church should be out where the unsaved are located: in business offices, in the marketplace, in shops, in your home—wherever you are. That is where the church does its work. That is what it means to tell the Good News and to be salt.

> I counsel thee to buy of me gold refined by fire, that thou mayest become rich; and white garments, that thou mayest clothe thyself, and that the shame of thy nakedness be not made manifest; And eyesalve to anoint thine eyes, that thou mayest see.
>
> Verse eighteen

The city was given over to trading, and Jesus addressed these merchants in their own language: He invited them to trade with Him. In His divine wisdom, He touched the pulse of their business life.

Theirs was an extensive business of money transactions. One of their prideful customs was never to issue tarnished money to their clients. Therefore, they would remelt the gold coins when they tarnished and resmelt them. The only way they could make the coins shiny was in the fire of the smelter.

Jesus counseled them to buy gold from Him. However long the process used for refining their gold, the Laodiceans could never attain the high standard that Jesus offered. He was offering them heavenly treasures. If they would just lose sight of earthly treasures, they could walk on streets of gold!

The glossy black-colored wool of Laodicea was famous, but Jesus offered them clothing of dazzling white if they could receive it. He had warned them of their nakedness and extorted them to clothe themselves with the garments He offered: divine righteousness was available to cover them like a robe and conceal their nudity of which they seemed so totally unaware.

The irony of Jesus' words was probably lost on the members of the church. The Laodiceans bragged of their spiritual insight, and Jesus bluntly declared that they were blind. In a city known for its eyesalve, they were unable to see spirituality. The self-complacency of the satisfied city had so affected the church that it had become blind to its shortcomings and needs. Yet, a new vision was still possible, for the great Physician offered His own remedy for the restoration of their spiritual sight.

"As many as I love, I reprove and chasten: but zealous therefore, and repent" (verse nineteen).

Nevertheless, the conditions existing in the church in Laodicea would not be tolerated indefinitely. Because He loved, the Lord Jesus threatened to rebuke and chasten His people with the objective of bringing them to an acknowledgment of their faults and leading them to repentance by His chastisement.

Unlike the other churches, the church in Laodicea suffered no persecution from the Jewish leaders or the imperial power. Religious prejudice was absent. The Lord accordingly sought to arouse His people to a change of attitude and a renewal of their earlier zeal and enthusiasm.

"Behold, I stand at the door and knock: if any man hear my voice and open the door, I will come in to him, and will sup with him, and he with me" (verse twenty).

Jesus will never force His way into our lives. He will never use trickery. He will come in only if invited. But He will stand at the door to our hearts and knock, and He will never give up. He patiently awaits our response to His invitation. Through sickness and sorrow, suffering and loss, through the Scriptures and through circumstances, those gentle taps still make themselves heard on the door of life. And the Lover of our souls stands and pleads for us to let Him in.

To the one who throws open the door and responds, He promises full communion. When Jesus finds the entry into our heart and life, eternal bliss and communion with God become the believer's reality. It is not until we experience His presence in our lives that we can experience true happiness.

"He that overcometh, I will give to him to sit down with me in my throne, as I also overcame, and sat down with my Father in his throne" (verse twenty-one).

To the overcomer, Jesus promises a place on His throne. There is room for you and me there. It is a mark of special favor to be given a seat of honor. Jesus has promised all of His people this honor. We will sit with Him and judge the twelve tribes, and we will judge angels. This is more than a temporary honor. It is one we will have for eternity.

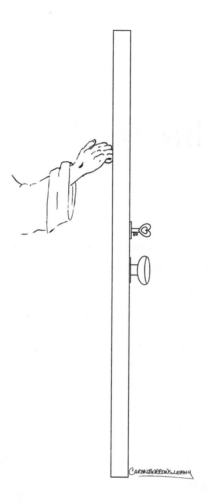

"He that hath an ear, let him hear what the Spirit saith to the churches" (verse twenty-two).

When Jesus repeated this call to each of the seven churches of Asia, it was not intended to be a meaningless repetition. He was calling upon Christians of all time to listen closely to what He had to say. This calls special attention to His messages, and they, and we, cannot ignore the messages of our Master.

Chapter Four

After these things I saw, and behold, a door opened in heaven, and the first voice that I heard, a voice as of a trumpet speaking with me, one saying, Come up hither, and I will show thee the things which must come to pass hereafter.

Verse one

Chapter four begins with these words: "After these things." The Greek words are *meta tauta*, which many English translators mistakenly translate as "after this." So, the question has to be raised, what things?

Going back to chapter one, verse nine, John was told to write the things that he had seen, the things which are, and the things that will occur in the future.

The "things that were" refer to those things John had been privy to prior to this revelation from Jesus. These were the events that John had been a part of while traveling with Jesus. "The things which are" refer to the events pertaining to the churches and the church period leading up to this interlude now introduced in chapter four.

The "things which are" came to a close at the end of chapter three. These "things" refer to the time from the beginning of Jesus' earthly ministry to the end of the historical church.

As we progress through the book of Revelation, you will note that from this point on, there is no further mention of the church until chapter nineteen, verse fourteen, when Jesus returns to the earth to set up His millennial kingdom. Until then, the Revelation account switches its location from earth to heaven and back several times. These switches are referred to as "interludes." Overall, we will see three major divisions: the Tribulation, the millennium, and the eternal state.

Back to chapter four: now, "after these things," John sees, in a vision, a view of heaven and God's glory through an opening that he calls a "door." This "door" allows him to see straight into the throne room of God. As he looks, a strong, loud voice commands him to come up to heaven. Here he is shown what will happen in the remainder of the history of the earth and its people.

"Straightway I was in the Spirit: and behold, there was a throne set in heaven, and one sitting upon the throne" (verse two).

In an instant, John was transported, in the Spirit, into the throne room of God. When John arrives there, he sees a figure sitting on the throne.

"And he that sat was to look upon like a jasper stone and a sardius: and there was a rainbow round about the throne, like an emerald to look upon" (verse three).

Notice that John doesn't try to describe the One sitting on the throne. He can only just try to describe the magnificence of the scene. The encircling brilliance of the glory of God is described by the only things that John knows about—blinding, bright light sparkling in the facets of precious gems: diamonds, rubies, and emeralds.

"And round about the throne were four and twenty thrones: and upon the thrones I saw four and twenty elders sitting, arrayed in white garments; and on their heads crowns of gold" (verse four).

John then notices twenty-four other figures present. They were each sitting on a throne of their own. There were twenty-four of them. He calls them the twenty-four elders. Each was wearing white clothing (white represents the righteousness of God). Each of them had a crown of gold on their head. The Greek language tells us that they were wearing stephanon, or "martyr's crowns," rather than "diadems," which are monarch's crowns. Who are these elders? There are at least thirteen different views on their identity. No one really knows. This is a question that we will have to be patient in waiting for an answer, and we may have to wait until the rapture.

"And out of the throne proceed lightnings and voices and thunders. And there were seven lamps of fire burning before the throne, which are the seven spirits of God" (verse five).

Lightning and thunder are physical signs of the coming storm. This storm is coming out of the throne of God. The storm speaks of the severe judgment that is too soon to follow. We had the angel's own interpretation of the seven lamps burning before the throne; they are the "seven spirits of God." These seven spirits are the angels, spirit beings that we will see next in Revelation 8:1–6. These are the seven angels who have the seven trumpets. More about this later! The voices are the voices of the heavenly creatures there with God.

"And before the throne, as it were a sea of glass like a crystal; and in the midst of the throne, and round about the throne, four living creatures full of eyes before and behind" (verse six).

The authors of nearly every book written on the Revelation come to the "sea of glass" and tend to spiritualize this "sea." I find it easier just to say I don't know what this signifies! The appearance is as if the sea was made of crystal. John didn't know, thus his use of the word, "like."

As to the four living creatures, when we examine John's description, we see that they were scattered all around the throne room. Comparing them to other creatures in Scripture, we find they have the same characteristics as the seraphim described in Isaiah 6:1–3. Here in Revelation, though, we see some additional features that were not described in Isaiah. These are heavenly beings of the highest order.

"And the first creature was like a lion, and the second creature like a calf, and the third creature had a face as of a man, and the fourth creature was like a flying eagle" (verse seven).

In this text, living creatures have faces not seen in the narrative in Isaiah. Each of the four creatures has a different characteristic. The first had features like a lion. The second head features of a calf. The third had features of a man, and the fourth had features of a flying eagle. Their duty is to be above the throne of God, glorifying Him.

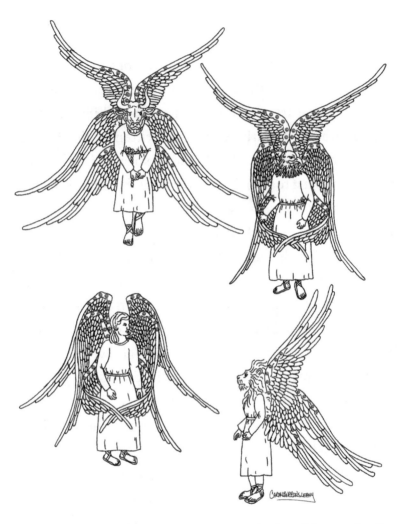

In Scripture, these animals are described as follows: the lion is defined as the king of the beasts, or royal power. The calf (ox) is a beast of burden, or the "servant animal." The man represents humanity. The eagle signifies God's realm of heaven. All of these are qualities of Jesus Christ. Matthew writes of Jesus' royalty (the lion) and pictures Him as king. Mark portrays Him as a servant (the calf or the ox). Luke as the Son of Man (the man's face), and John as Deity (the eagle).

And the four living creatures, having each one of
them six wings, are full of eyes round about and
within: and they have no rest day and night, saying,
Holy, holy, holy, is the Lord God, the Almighty, who
was and who is and who is to come.

Verse eight

Day and night, these living creatures praise God, saying,
"Holy, holy, holy is the Lord God Almighty." And they include
words that attribute to His eternality: "Who was, who is, and
who is to come"! This describes the fact that the Lord Jesus
Christ is the object of worship in heaven. He is the One who
sits on the throne and is the object of their affection.

Each of these creatures has six wings. They are one of two
heavenly creatures with wings. They are seraphim (seraphs).
The only other heavenly creature with wings is the cherub, who
has four wings. There is one other winged creature in Scripture, in Zechariah 5:9. These are described as "two women, and
the wind was in their wings; for they had wings like the wings
of a stork" (Zechariah 5:9, KJV).

Some have identified these "women" as angels, but in Greek,
they are not *angelos*, or angels, but in the Septuagint version
of Zechariah, the term used is *gunaikes*, which is translated as
"women." *Gunaikes* is the Greek word from which we get our
English word "gynecology." Further, these flying "women" were
associated with, and protective of, the woman in the ephah
(basket), of whom the angel said, "This is Wickedness" (Zechariah 5:8). We can be sure that they are agents of evil because of

their association with this "woman." And come as I said before: angels do not have wings. In every mention of angels in Scripture, angels have the appearance of a man. Also, the Greek term angelos is in the Greek masculine gender.

And one last comment: storks are always said to be an "unclean" bird (see: Leviticus 11:19), and God does not allow uncleanness in heaven (with the exception of Satan, who will have access to God's throne until the middle of the Tribulation period).

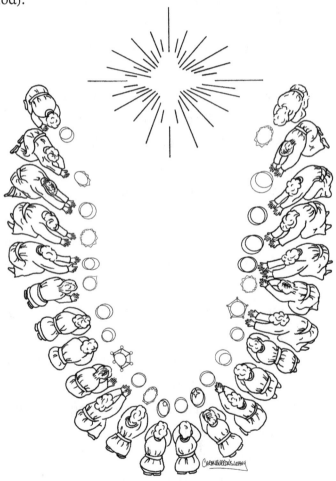

And when the living creatures shall give glory and honor and thanks to him that sitteth on the throne, to him that liveth for ever and ever, the four and twenty elders shall fall down before him that sitteth on the throne, and shall worship in him that liveth for ever and ever, and shall cast their crowns before the throne.

Verses nine to ten

As the living creatures give honor to Jesus Christ, the elders prostrate themselves before Him, worshipping Him. As a part of the worship, they take off their crowns and throw them at His feet. Their worship has a special significant meaning. They testified that if it had not been for Jesus, they could not have the victory over sin and death. By His sacrifice, they, like we, were saved.

"Saying Worthy art thou, our Lord and our God, to receive the glory and the honor and the power: for thou didst create all things, and because of thy will they were, and were created" (verse eleven).

By anticipating the ultimate consummation of history, chapter four reveals a glimpse of heaven where all of God's created beings join in a symphony of praise and give honor and worship to our almighty God.

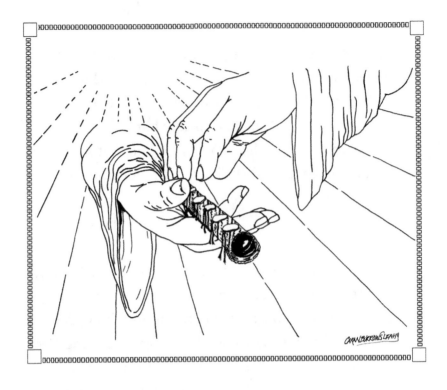

Chapter Five

"And I saw in the right hand of him that sat on the throne a book written within and on the back, close sealed with seven seals" (verse one).

In this chapter, John is introduced to an item of extreme importance, namely a scroll. The scroll is the correct term, not "book"! This scroll was held in the right hand of the One sitting on the throne. The fact that it was held in the right hand is significant since the right hand is the hand of power. Another important factor is that the scroll is written on both sides of the material of the scroll. Furthermore, the scroll is sealed with seven seals.

"And I saw a strong angel proclaiming with a great voice, Who is worthy to open the book, and to loose the seals thereof?" (verse two).

John's attention is focused on the scroll when he hears a strong angel voicing a question loudly. This angel is using a great voice, which signifies a herald, and the great voice gives urgency to this question: "Who is worthy to open the scroll and break the wax seals that hold its secrets within?" This question demands an authoritative answer.

"And no one in the heaven, or on the earth, or under the earth, was able to open the book, or to look thereon" (verse three).

It is obvious that whoever is worthy must be someone of great importance and with great authority. It is evident that the contents of this scroll are impressive and require the power of God for their revelation and the execution of their program.

"And I wept much, because no one was found worthy to open the book, or to look thereon" (verse four).

John cries because, in all of creation, no one is found worthy to open the scroll and see its contents.

"And one of the elders saith unto me, Weep not; behold, the Lion that is of the tribe of Judah, the Root of David, hath overcome to open the book and the seven seals thereof" (verse five).

One of the twenty-four elders who surround the throne now says to John: "Stop crying; there is Someone who can open the scroll! He is the Lion of Judah!" This is a reference to Genesis 49:9–10, where it is prophesied that the future ruler of the earth will come from the tribe of Judah, the lion tribe. This is a reference to Jesus, who is declared to be "the Root of David." This stems from the prophecy of Isaiah 11:10 (KJV), which says, "And there shall come forth a rod out of the stem of Jesse, and a Branch shall grow out of his roots."

This "Lion" has a victory of some kind that signifies that He has the right to take the scroll, open it, and break the seals. This implies that Jesus is completely worthy and has full authority and sovereignty in respect to the contents of the seven-sealed scroll.

And I saw in the midst of the throne and of the four living creatures, and in the midst of the elders, a Lamb standing, as though it had been slain, having seven horns, and seven eyes, which are the seven Spirits of God, sent forth into all the earth.

Verse six

In the center of the brilliance of the light around the throne, John sees a figure standing at the throne. This figure is surrounded by the four living creatures and the twenty-four elders. As his eyes focus on the brilliant light, John recognizes the figure as that of a sacrificial lamb. Since the lamb is standing, this description suggests that it had been resurrected from the dead. The seven horns and the seven eyes represent the seven spirits of God that would be sent around the earth. These seven spirits are the same angels that we saw in Revelation 4:5.

"And he came, and he taketh it out of the right hand of him that sat on the throne" (verse seven).

Then the Lamb takes the scroll out of the right hand of the Person sitting on the throne. The One sitting on the throne is clearly God the Father. In the act of taking the scroll, it is made evident that judgment and power over the earth are committed to Jesus Christ, the Son of God. Daniel 7:13–14 is a parallel passage. There Daniel reveals the ultimate triumph of Jesus when the kingdoms of the world are given to Him. Daniel declares,

I saw in the night-visions, and, behold, there came with the clouds of heaven one like unto a son of man, and he came even to the ancient of days, and they brought him near before him. And there was given [to] him dominion, and glory, and a kingdom, that all the peoples, nations, and languages should serve him: his domination is an everlasting dominion, which shall not pass away, and his kingdom that which shall not be destroyed.

Daniel 7:13–14

In that future day, complete authority over the earth will be realized by Jesus, an authority that He will exercise both in the judgments that precede His second coming and in His reign for 1,000 years, and whose glory will continue throughout eternity.

And when he had taken the book, the four living creatures and the four and twenty elders fell down before the Lamb, having each one a harp, and golden bowls full of incense, which are the prayers of the saints.

Verse eight

The importance of the scene is shown by the reaction of the four living creatures and the twenty-four elders. Falling down prostrate before the Lamb, they begin to worship. Each of them has a lyre, or small harp. Apart from the trumpet, the lyre is the only instrument mentioned in heavenly worship. There is no mention of them being played at this time, but this is the implication.

The golden bowls (Greek: *phials*) are shallow bowls used when pouring out a liquid during worship in the Temple. These golden bowls are said to hold the prayers of the saints and have the aroma of incense. Incense was used in the Temple when prayers were lifted to God. David said, in Psalm 141:2, "Let my prayer be set forth as incense before thee"; the role of the elders is that of lifting up the prayers of the saints.

> And they sing a new song, saying, Worthy art thou to take the book, and to open the seals thereof: for thou was slain, and didst purchase unto God with thy blood men of every tribe, and tongue, and people, and nation.
>
> Verse nine

Along with their worship and the use of the lyres and incense, they sing a new song in which Jesus Christ is said to be worthy to open the scroll because of His work of redemption throughout all of mankind, which He affected with His own blood.

In my comment on the twenty-four elders in Revelation 4:4, I stated that there were many different views on just who these twenty-four elders were. Here we see some additional information. Here they declare in their "new song" that they are representing the saints.

"And madest them to be unto our God a kingdom and priests; and they reign upon earth" (verse ten).

The "priests" are the church! This confirms the promise made by Jesus in the letter to the church in Laodicea: "He that overcometh, I will give to him to sit down with me in my throne, as I also overcame, and sat down with my Father in his throne"

(Revelation 3:21). When we go to be with the Lord, we will share everything with Him. We will be joint heirs, and as joint heirs, we will forever be joined to Jesus. Where He goes, we will go. What He does, we will do. We will share His glory, and we will share His sovereign rule.

> And I saw, and I heard a voice of many angels round about the throne and the living creatures and the elders; and the number of them was ten thousand times ten thousand, and thousands of thousands.
>
> Verse eleven

John sees a remarkable scene: around the throne of God and around the living creatures and the twenty-four elders appeared a huge number of angels. John uses the Hebrew way of saying that there were so many of them that they were uncountable. The Jews had no number above ten thousand. If they wanted to indicate such a large number, well above ten thousand, they would say, "ten thousand times ten thousand." Here John adds up even more to the count. He adds, "and thousands of thousands." In English, we probably don't have a number that large either. Let it stay as a huge number of angels there around God's throne.

John then records their loud chant: "Saying with a great voice, Worthy is the Lamb that hath been slain to receive the power, and riches, and wisdom, and might and honor, and glory, and blessing" (verse twelve).

The sevenfold attributes ascribed to the Lamb sum up their worship and adoration. This chorus of angels is the prelude to the scenes that will begin to unfold.

And every created thing which is in the heaven, and on the earth, and under the earth, and on the sea, and all things are in them, heard I saying, Unto him that sitteth on the throne, and unto the Lamb, be the blessing, and the honor, and the glory, and the dominion, forever and ever.

Verse thirteen

Added to this great chorus in heaven is the praise of every creature on the earth, under the earth, and in the sea. If I read this correctly, every man, woman, child, animal, and marine specimen, join in with the living creatures, the twenty-four elders, and the angelic host and praise the Lamb who is sitting on the throne, climaxing the scene of worship.

"And the four living creatures said, Amen. And the elders fell down and worshiped" (verse fourteen).

As a final note, the twenty-four elders once again prostrate themselves before the throne of God.

All of creation's praise came because the Lamb took the scroll from the Father's hand. God's great eternal plan could now be set free from the bondage of sin and death.

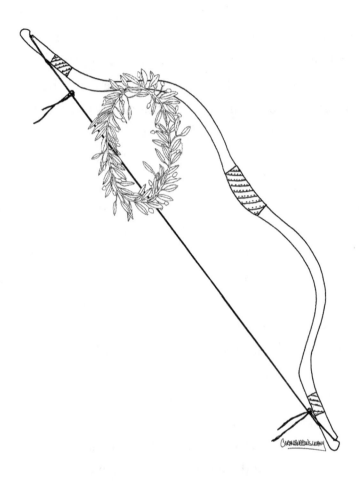

Chapter Six

"And I saw when the Lamb opened one of the seven seals, and I heard one of the four living creatures saying as with the voice of thunder, Come" (verse one).

In chapters four and five, we were in heaven with John. Here in chapter six, we see the scene shifting. The Lamb breaks open the first seal of the scroll. One of the four living creatures says, in a loud voice, "Come!" This is an invitation to John to follow along. There is something John is to see and record. John is transported back to the earth in the future.

"And I saw, and behold, a white horse, and he that sat thereon had a bow; and there was given unto him a crown: and he came forth conquering, and to conquer" (verse two).

John now sees a white horse. In Scripture and in the Orient in ancient times, the white horse was a symbol of victory. The rider of a white horse is the victor. There is one thing here that is different from the victory ride of a conqueror. In antiquity, the victor always has a sword in his right hand. The right hand signifies strength, and the sword represents the victor's strength over his enemy. This rider holds a bow, not a sword. Then, the rider is given a crown. The crown he was given is a *stephanon*, or victor's crown. This is not the crown of royalty (Greek: *diadema*) because this crown belongs only to the Son of God.

There are those who would have this rider be Jesus, but Jesus is the One who is breaking open the seals, so it cannot be Him! When Jesus comes riding a white horse (Revelation 19:11–16), He will come with a sharp sword proceeding out of His mouth with which He will strike down the nations, not a bow. When He comes, He will come as a warrior and not a victor. His victory will come later, as we will see in the text of Revelation.

And about the bow of this rider: this rider has no arrows! Even though he comes to conquer, there will be no warfare in his victory and no fighting. His victory is one of consent, not bloodshed. In other words, this conqueror is given his crown; he does not earn it. Yet, he will wage war and will conquer his enemies. Who are the enemies? We will see this at a later time.

"And when he opened the second seal, I heard the second living creature saying, Come" (verse three).

Jesus now opens the second seal of the seven-sealed scroll. The second living creature gives John another command to come. John again follows.

> And another horse came forth, a red horse: and to him that sat thereon it was given to take peace from the earth, and that they should slay one another: and there was given unto him a great sword.
>
> Verse four

This time the color of the horse John sees is red. The rider was given the right to take away peace from the earth. This phrase is significant because after the first rider has come, there is peace on the earth. Unfortunately, this peace is short-lived. Quickly, the people of the earth are at war! There would be bloodshed, as indicated by the color of the horse. The rider of this horse was given a large sword representing wanton bloodshed.

"And when he opened the third seal, I heard the third living creature saying, Come. And I saw, and behold, a black horse; and he that sat thereon had a balance in his hand" (verse five).

Once more, Jesus breaks a seal on the seven-sealed scroll. This third seal ushers in a rider on a black horse. John records that this rider has a balance scale in his hand.

The color black is often connected with famine. Famine and war go hand in hand. During times of war and bloodshed, food is usually hard to find. Most of the available food goes to feed the troops, and civilians are left without.

Significant is the scale held in this rider's hand. Food shortages always drive prices up.

"And I heard as it were a voice in the midst of the four living creatures saying, A measure of wheat for a shilling, and three measures of barley for a shilling; and the oil and the wine hurt thou not" (verse six).

There is an old Jewish phrase, which is used when food is scarce: "To eat bread by weight." This signifies that bread is worth its weight in money. This living creature cries out, "A measure of wheat for a denarius, and three measures of barley for a denarius."

A denarius was the standard day's wage for a laborer. A measure of wheat was about the equivalent of two pints, just enough to make bread for one person. It takes three times as much barley to be the equivalent of wheat. Therefore, a man would have to work all day just to have enough bread for himself. There would be nothing left for a family. At the same time, the rich would be enjoying plenty, as represented by the oil and wine. The angel was not to touch the oil and wine.

"And when he opened the fourth seal, I heard the voice of the fourth living creature saying, Come" (verse seven).

Again, John hears the command, "Come!"

> And I saw, and behold, a pale horse: and he that sat upon him, his name was Death; and Hades followed with him. And there was given unto them authority over the fourth part of the earth, to kill with sword, and with famine, and with death, and by the wild beasts of the earth.
>
> Verse eight

This time John sees a pale horse. This horse had death for a rider. Following right behind him was Hades, or hell. Death claims the body, and hell claims the soul. John saw these two enemies going forth to claim their prey after the carnage of the sword and famine. When death and hell had finished, the wild beasts would join in on the carnage.

"And when he opened the fifth seal, I saw underneath the altar the souls of them that had been slain for the word of God, and for the testimony which they held" (verse nine).

In the Old Testament, when a priest presented an animal for sacrifice, the blood of the sacrifice was poured out at the base of the brazen altar. In the Old Testament imagery, blood represents life. So here, the image of the souls of the martyrs "underneath the altar" indicates that these were ones whose lives were given sacrificially to the glory of God. They had become martyrs because they testified for Jesus Christ. Their testimony had become their death sentence.

"And they cried with a great voice, saying, How long, O Master, the holy and true, dost thou not judge and avenge our blood on them that dwell on the earth?" (verse ten).

The question asked here is not whether their killers would be avenged, but *when*. "How long" has been the cry of God's suffering people throughout the ages. The saints in heaven know that God will eventually judge sin and establish righteousness on the earth, but as to when, no one knows God's schedule.

Today, when we say the Lord's Prayer, we are asking for the same thing. "Thy kingdom come; Thy will be done on earth as it is in heaven." God's kingdom cannot come until the Tribulation period has run its course.

> And there was given [to] them each one a white robe; and it was said unto them, that they should rest yet for a little time, until their fellow-servants also and their brethren, who should be killed even as they were, should have fulfilled their course.
>
> Verse eleven

A white robe is the symbol of righteousness. These martyrs are clearly believers. They are God's people, and God makes it clear that He will avenge His people. But at this time, there are still those on the earth who belong to Him who will be slain for their faith. Meanwhile, the martyrs are to sit back and wait until the rest of those who are witnessing for God finish their work.

"And I saw when he opened the sixth seal, and there was a great earthquake; and the sun became black as sackcloth of hair, and the whole moon became as blood" (verse twelve).

At this time, John saw the Lamb open the sixth seal. The opening of this seal would usher in worldwide catastrophes, including the first of three great earthquakes. All of nature is to be affected: the sun, the moon, the stars, the mountains, and the islands.

Even though John uses symbolic language, these verses describe a scene that will frighten even the bravest of people. The sun will not shine, and the moon will turn bloodred.

"And the stars of the heaven fell unto the earth, as a fig tree casteth her unripe figs when she is shaken of a great wind" (verse thirteen).

Stars will fall to the earth, like green figs falling off the fig tree when a gale-force wind blows. We know now that the stars are actually other suns, and if they would suddenly fall on the earth, the earth would be destroyed, but from the standpoint of ancient cosmology, this scene is one of a major catastrophe.

"And the heaven was removed as a scroll when it is rolled up; and every mountain and island were moved out of their places" (verse fourteen).

Looking up to the sky, a person on this day would see the stars disappear like a line of words disappears when a scroll is rolled up. This picture of God's judgment is terrifying. This is, to use the common terms, to say, "all hell breaks loose!" Every feature on the earth will change. Mountains will be leveled, and islands will be displaced.

Without a doubt, this describes an earthquake of proportions never known before. In ancient times, earthquakes were viewed as proof of divine wrath and judgment, but these earthquakes give abundant evidence that something apocalyptic is taking place.

In the face of such devastation, those living at this time will be terrorized.

"And the kings of the earth, and the princes, and the chief captains, and the rich, and the strong, and every bondman and freeman, hid themselves in the caves and in the rocks of the mountains" (verse fifteen).

These verses show the error that all classes of people will have at this time. God's judgment will fall on all of those who refuse to repent. These people will run and try to hide from God by going into caves and hiding behind rocks in the mountains.

"And they say to the mountains and to the rocks, Fall on us, and hide us from the face of him that sitteth on the throne, and from the wrath of the Lamb" (verse sixteen).

This verse always baffles me. From the way it is worded, all of these people know that God's wrath is falling on them, and yet, they refuse to repent. They would rather hide in a hole in the ground than run to Him in faith. Imagine wanting to hide from the Lamb.

Rank and wealth will not save anyone on that terrible day. God's wrath is not like a child's temper tantrum or punishment given by an impatient parent. God's wrath is the evidence of His holy love for all that is right and His holy hatred for all that is evil in the world.

"For the great day of their wrath is come; and who is able to stand?" (verse seventeen).

Again, I am amazed these people will know that God's wrath is being poured out on them and yet, will not admit that they are sinners in dire need of a Savior. They know that there is nothing they can do to save themselves, and yet they will not rely on the only One who can save them.

All of the events of this chapter can be explained away by those who are unbelievers. We have had wars almost continually for thousands of years. In my lifetime, I have seen WW II, Korea, Vietnam, Afghanistan, Gulf War, the war in Iraq, and many other conflicts around the world. Since WW II, we have had troops stationed around the world all the time, so unbelievers will just look at war as something that happens all the time.

There have always been famines around the world in every generation, so famine is nothing new.

As for diseases, every year, we see new diseases or new strains of diseases, so that's nothing new.

But here, at the end of chapter six, we see that those unbelievers finally understand that God's wrath has been unleashed upon them.

They finally recognize that something spoken of centuries before has come to pass: *the great day of God's wrath* has come!

There are over one hundred passages in the Old Testament that appear under such terms as the day of the Lord's wrath, the day of the Lord's anger, the day of vengeance, the time of the Lord's vengeance, and the day of God's wrath (Zephaniah 1:15, 18; 2:2–3; Proverbs 6:34; Jeremiah 51:6; Isaiah 61:2; 63:4). In the New Testament, some twenty terms are used in describing the future day of the Lord. All of the prophets have written, in their various terminologies, what the last days have in store for both believers and unbelievers.

Chapter six concludes the events of the first three and a half years of the Tribulation period. Each of the events that have been covered, from chapter four to the end of chapter six, can be explained as natural events. For instance: since the dawn of time, there have been wars. There have also been earthquakes, famines, and diseases.

But from this point on, the upcoming events cannot be considered to be from natural causes. Those who are on the earth finally come to the realization that what has happened has not been natural but is God's wrath. Additionally, they are brought to the point where they know that God's wrath is being poured out upon the earth.

All seven of the years of God's wrath are called the Tribulation. The last three and a half years are referred to as the Great Tribulation. This coincides with Jeremiah 30:7, which speaks of the "time of Jacob's trouble," and Matthew 24:21–22, which calls this time the "Great Tribulation."

Chapter seven is designated as an interlude. Chapter seven resumes with the opening of the seals of the scroll.

The Lost Tribes of Israel

Although the phrase "the lost tribes of Israel" emits a certain aura of mystery that romanticizes the disappearance of the Jews taken into captivity by Assyria in 722 BC, this is never mentioned in Scripture.

It is false teaching known as British Israelism.

British Israelism, or Anglo-Israelism, came into existence only 150 years ago. An Englishman, Richard Brothers (1757–1824), is given the dubious distinction of originating his own method of biblical interpretation, which is theological anti-semitism that says that the Anglo-Saxon people are, in fact, Israel. Consequently, the British are the true heirs of all God's promises to the Jewish nation.

His perversion of the Bible was picked up by Herbert W. Armstrong, who is the founder of the Worldwide Church of God, which we now know is a godless cult. Today, the Worldwide Church of God claims that these Jews transferred from Jerusalem to England and that Queen Elizabeth is a direct descendant of David and sits on the throne of Israel, continuing David's dynasty. This is the very throne on which Jesus Christ will sit after His return. It is claimed that the United States, an offshoot of England, is included in this false teaching, and together England and the United States are the "lost tribes."

Chapter Seven

The last verse of chapter six ends with "the great day of their wrath is come." This *great wrath* is the wrath that is recorded in Matthew 24:21 and Daniel 9: 21. Now we see another interlude, where the scene shifts once more.

"After this I saw four angels standing at the four corners of the earth, holding the four winds of the earth, that no wind should blow on the earth, or on the sea, or upon on any tree" (verse one).

The expression "the four corners of the earth" was used in antiquity just as we use "the four points of the compass." This expression simply says that God has placed His four messengers to cover the earth.

These four messengers have been given the power to still the winds. There is not even a slight breeze to put a ripple on the surface of the seas or to make the leaves on a tree rustle.

And I saw another angel ascend from the sunrising, having the seal of the living God: and he cried with a great voice to the four angels to whom it was given to hurt the earth and the sea, saying, Hurt not the earth,

neither the sea, nor the trees, till we shall have sealed
the servants of our God on their foreheads.

Verses two to three

This angel from the sunrising, or from the east, gives the
previous four angels orders to hold back the winds until the
servants of God have been marked on their foreheads by the
other angels.

From the language here, it seems that after God's servants
have received the special mark on their foreheads, the four angels will let the stilled winds blow again and that these winds
will be bringing destruction on the earth, the seas, and the
trees.

"And I heard the number of them that were sealed, a hundred and forty and four thousand, sealed out of every tribe of
the children of Israel" (verse four).

These 144,000 who receive the seal of God are all Jews (the
children of Israel). They come from the twelve tribes of Israel.

Of the tribe of Judah were sealed twelve thousand:
Of the tribe of Reuben twelve thousand; Of the tribe
of Gad twelve thousand; of the tribe of Asher twelve
thousand; Of the tribe of Naphtali twelve thousand;
Of the tribe of Manasseh twelve thousand; of the
tribe of Simeon twelve thousand; Of the tribe of Levi
twelve thousand; Of the tribe of Issachar twelve thousand; of the tribe of Zebulun twelve thousand; Of the
tribe of Joseph twelve thousand; Of the tribe of Benjamin were sealed twelve thousand.

Verses five to eight

John goes even farther. He lists the number of those who are sealed as being 12,000 from each of the twelve tribes of Israel. John omits the original tribes of Dan and Ephraim.

There have been many efforts to solve this seeming enigma, especially to solve the absence of the tribes of Dan and Ephraim. This is due to the fact that these two tribes were notorious for their fickleness and bent toward idol worship. In his Palestinian covenant, God warned His people that if any man, woman, family, or tribe turn from the Lord to serve the idols of the nations, He would "blot out his name from under heaven [and] [...] separate him unto evil out of all the tribes of Israel" (Deuteronomy 29:20–21, KJV).

In less than half a century after this warning, the tribe of Dan set up a graven image (Judges 18:30), and later, a prophet wrote, "Ephraim is joined to idols; let him alone" (Hosea 4:17). Zechariah says in 13:8 (KJV), "And it shall come to pass, that in all the land, saith the LORD, two parts therein shall be cut off and die; but the third shall be left therein." Therefore, both of these tribes have been cut off from the nation of Israel by God because of idolatry.

At the beginning of the nation of Israel, the tribe of Levi was designated the priestly tribe. They were interspersed among the other tribes and were not given a tribal distinction. Now, since all followers of Jesus are considered to be "kings and priests unto God," with Jesus as the High Priest (Revelation 1:6; 5:10; Hebrews 3:1; 4:14–15; 7:21; 8:1; 9:11), there is no longer a need for the priestly tribe. Therefore, the tribe of Levi will take a normal tribal position in the new Israel.

Joseph was given a "double portion" in the nation, and after His death, this portion was divided between Manasseh and Ephraim, his sons.

> After these things I saw, and behold, a great multitude, which no man could number, out of every nation and of all tribes and peoples and tongues, standing before the throne and before the Lamb, arrayed in white robes, and palms in their hands.
>
> Verse nine

Again, John sees a great, uncountable number of people standing before the throne of God and before Jesus Christ. They came from every nation on the earth, from the entire world population. They are clothed in white robes and carry palm fronds in their hands. Their clothing indicates that they have been cleansed from sin. White clothing symbolizes righteousness, which only comes from salvation through Jesus Christ.

The palms in their hands denote victory and rejoicing. This word, "palms," is only used two times in the New Testament. Here, and during the triumphal entry of Jesus into Jerusalem in John 12:13.

"And they cry with a great voice, saying, Salvation unto our God who sitteth on the throne, and unto the Lamb" (verse ten).

This great multitude of people cheer as loud as they can, praising God and Jesus Christ for their salvation. They indicate that the source of their salvation is God the Father through the Lamb of Calvary.

And all the angels were standing round about the throne, and about the elders and the four living creatures; and they fell before the throne on their faces, and worshiped God, saying, Amen: Blessing, and glory, and wisdom, and thanksgiving, and honor, and power, and might, be unto our God forever and ever. Amen.

Verses eleven to twelve

As they did in Revelation 5:11–12, the angels followed the multitude in a sevenfold adoration. Except for the word "riches" (replaced by "thanksgiving"), their praise is identical. Of note also is the fact that the angels prostrate themselves before the throne.

"And one of the elders answered, saying unto me, These that are arrayed in white robes, who are they, and whence came they?" (verse thirteen).

One of the elders asks John who these people in the white robes are and where they came from.

"And I say into him, My lord, thou knowest. And he said to me, These are they that come of the great tribulation, and they washed their robes, and made them white in the blood of the Lamb" (verse fourteen).

John's answer implied that he didn't know who they were. How could he? He realized that the elder was leading him, but he just didn't know the answer to his question. He did realize that the elder knew, and with his curiosity aroused, said as much.

The elder then told John who the people were. They were the martyred witnesses for God who were slain during the first half of the Tribulation period. Their blood was shed because they stood up for God. These were killed in warfare, in starvation, by disease, etc.

"Therefore are they before the throne of God; and they serve him day and night in his temple: and he that sitteth on the throne shall spread his tabernacle over them" (verse fifteen).

As these people continue on in the presence of God, they will be with Him, serve Him, and worship Him, and He will shelter them.

"They shall hunger no more, neither thirst any more; neither shall the sun strike upon them, nor any heat" (verse sixteen).

In their new environment, they will never experience hunger or thirst, nor will they be exposed to any of the elements.

"For the Lamb that is in the midst of the throne shall be their shepherd, and shall guide them unto fountains of waters of life: and God shall wipe away every tear from their eyes" (verse seventeen).

Jesus will be their shepherd. He will provide for their every need. They will have no fear, no worries, no health problems, no heartaches, forever.

Chapter Eight

"And when he opened the seventh seal, there followed a silence in heaven about the space of half an hour" (verse one).

After the episodes of chapter seven, which mainly pertain to the sealing of the 144,000, the seal judgments are now resumed. But before John has the contents shown to him, there is complete silence in heaven for half an hour.

In order to account for this silence, we have to understand that something very unusual and of tremendous importance is about to take place. The silence is in direct contrast to what we have seen before, with all of the heavenly creation loudly praising God, and even the cherubim are said to be singing, "Holy, holy, holy, Lord God almighty."

The scroll has now been opened completely and perhaps even been turned over. It seemed as though the heavenly hosts were awestruck by what they were seeing.

So then, why this strange silence? We know that God's patience is not exhausted. When the sixth seal was opened, nature responded with a mighty convulsion, and brave men weakened for a moment. Jesus Christ used this time to give them the opportunity to repent, but when the heat let up, they went back to their old blasphemous ways.

Someone once said, "The steps of God from mercy to judgment are always slow, reluctant, and measured." God is reluctant to judge, for He is slow to anger. But this silence is the transition from grace to judgment.

As in the opening of the previous six seals, John receives another vision revealing the contents of this section of the scroll.

"And I saw the seven angels that stand before God; and there were given unto them seven trumpets" (verse two).

A new vision begins here. During this silence, the seven angels, who were mentioned in Revelation 1:4, 3:1, 4:5, and 5:6, were each given a trumpet. Trumpets were significant to the Jews. They were blown to call the people together; they announced war, and they announced special times. For instance, they were sounded at Mount Sinai when the Law was given; they were blown when a king was anointed, and everyone knows about the trumpets blown at the conquest of Jericho, and even here in Revelation, a trumpet was sounded to summon John to heaven (Revelation 4:1). Trumpets were also used in another situation: they were used to announce defeat and retreat.

Therefore, the seventh seal contains the seven trumpets. Sounding seven trumpets would be enough to announce the declaration of war against the minions of the devil and would announce a charge that would lead to the defeat of all of his followers.

And another angel came and stood over the altar, having a gold censer; And there was given unto him much incense, that he should add it unto the prayers of all the saints upon the golden altar which was before the throne.

Verse three

Now a different angel comes. The altar where the angel stands with the golden censer before the throne of God is the brazen altar, the altar of sacrifice. This is where the martyrs have been crying, "How long will it be before we are avenged?" Burning incense is used to give a sweet smell to the offering. Prayer for us today, in order to be acceptable, must be in the name of Jesus Christ. He offered Himself as a sacrifice to God, "for a sweetsmelling savour" (Ephesians 5:2, KJV). Thus the incense renders the prayers effective.

"And the smoke of the incense, with the prayers of the saints, went up before God out of the angel's hand" (verse four).

The angel has lit the incense, and as it burns, smoke begins to rise up to God. The smoke contains the prayers of the followers of Jesus Christ.

"And the angel taketh the censer; and he filled it with the fire of the altar and cast it upon the earth: and there followed thunders, and voices, and lightnings, and an earthquake" (verse five).

The angel now takes the censer, fills it with fire from the brazen altar, and throws it from heaven down to the earth. As the fire rains down, it is accompanied by thunder, voices, and lightning. As you know, thunder is a signal of an approaching storm. The voices are not defined as to their origin. But they are a warning to those on the earth. The lightning suggests that what is happening is happening very quickly. The earth quakes at the ferocity of this storm and the outrage of heaven.

"And the seven angels that had the seven trumpets prepared themselves to sound" (verse six).

It should be noted once more before we proceed that the seventh seal contains the seven trumpets. We see now that the seven angels who were given the seven trumpets are now making ready to execute their part in God's judgment of the people of the earth.

Again, looking back to chapter six, verse seventeen, those on the earth are aware that the great wrath of God has been unleashed on them. The horrible events of the first six seals will seem like nothing compared to what is to come. Since I have read the entire book many times, I know that from this point on, everything will proceed very rapidly.

We are now midway into the Tribulation period!

> And the first sounded, and there followed hail and fire, mingled with blood, and they were cast upon the earth: and the third part of the earth was burnt up, and the third part of the trees was burnt up, and all green grass was burnt up.
>
> Verse seven

This first trumpet judgment resembles the seventh plague of Egypt when hail and fire mingled and fell on the earth and killed every herb and tree in Egypt except those in Goshen. This judgment, though, falls on the entire earth, and one-third of all of the worldwide vegetation is destroyed in an instant by the fire mingled with blood. Not only was there smoke all over the world from the fires—but can you imagine the smell of burnt blood?

"And the second angel sounded, and as it were a great mountain burning with fire was cast into the sea: and a third part of the sea became blood" (verse eight).

When this second angel blows the trumpet, a mass as big as a mountain falls into the sea. It was aflame and turned one-third of the seas into blood. Since the seas cover one-seventh of the earth's surface, that means that a lot of water will be polluted! Many people have tried to change this "mountain" into a meteor, but this is a supernatural event and uses supernatural materials for a supernatural judgment. How this mountain-size mass will turn one-third of the world's oceans into blood is beyond our comprehension, but the Bible records it as Jesus' revelation to John, and that makes it true, believe it or not.

"And there died the third part of the creatures which were in the sea, even they that had life; and the third part of the ships was destroyed" (verse nine).

As the seawater turns to blood, it kills one-third of all of the sea creatures, and not only that—one-third of the ships at sea are destroyed. Again, this is almost beyond belief, but it will happen!

"And the third angel sounded, and there fell from heaven a great star, burning as a torch, and it fell upon the third part of the rivers, and upon the fountains of the waters" (verse ten).

Now that one-third of the seawaters have been destroyed, the third angel blows his trumpet and brings forth a star from heaven, which burns like a torch. This star falls on the fresh water of the rivers, streams, and springs.

"And the name of the star is called Wormwood: and the third part of the waters became wormwood; And many men died of the waters, because they were made bitter" (verse eleven).

This star has a name, Wormwood. This "wormwood" causes the water to become bitter, and when people drink this water, it kills them. The Greek word for "wormwood" is translated into English as "absinth," which literally means "undrinkable." This is the same absinth that is an alcoholic drink, also illegal to have in the US.

Many people will die from drinking this bitter water, but with one-third of the potable water gone, people would become desperate for drinking water, especially in the dry desert areas of the world. In WW II, many sailors died from drinking seawater when their ships were sunk, and they were set afloat in life rafts with no fresh water. This single result of the trumpet judgments will be highly significant to those people involved.

> And the fourth angel sounded, and the third part of the sun was smitten, and the third part of the moon, and the third part of the stars; that the third part of them should be darkened, and the day should not shine for the third part of it, and the night in like manner.
>
> Verse twelve

If you are following, you will note that there is a progression here. With this trumpet, one-third of the vegetation, one-third of the seas, marine life, shipping, and one-third of the heavenly bodies are gone! Food is destroyed; transportation is crippled; the water supply is diminished; one-third of the sunlight and moonlight has disappeared. Cold creeps in, and gloom is everywhere. Time goes on, but there is a definite limitation of everything man needs to survive.

> And I saw, and I heard an eagle, flying in the mid heaven, saying with a great voice, Woe, woe, woe, for them that dwell on the earth, by reason of the other voices of the trumpet of the three angels, who are yet to sound.
>
> Verse thirteen

After this fourth trumpet has sounded, an announcement is made by an eagle, who delivers an ominous message. Please note, if your Bible translation says "angel," this is not an angel flying; it is an eagle! The Greek word used is aetou, not angelos! This eagle has a very loud voice. Some say the eagles cannot talk. Well, masses as big as mountains on fire cannot come flying out of the sky either, can they? Well, they can if God is causing it to happen!

The message is a proclamation! If you think the first four trumpets are bad, just wait until you see what the last three have in store! This is a solemn warning of what is to come. There are three "woes" to come. There is one "woe" for each of the remaining three trumpets, which have yet to be blown.

A *woe* is a great calamity. And a calamity means destruction. Again, I have to note that everything we have seen so far is mild compared to what is coming!

Chapter Nine

"And the fifth angel sounded, and I saw a star from heaven fallen unto the earth: and there was given to him the key of the pit of the abyss" (verse one).

When the fifth angel blew his trumpet, a "star" "fell" from heaven to the earth. Many people think that this is a heavenly body like our sun. All stars are bigger than the earth, and if it were one of the celestial masses, it would completely destroy the earth. But it is not! A star is one category of many heavenly creatures. We see mention of these beings listed in Job 38:7, where it says, "When the morning stars sang together, all of the sons of God shouted for joy." We will soon see some other heavenly beings as we proceed through this book.

It seems obvious that this star is trusted with the key to the gateway of this abyss. He is given the job of opening this fiendish place, which is filled with demonic creatures, as we see in the next verse.

"And he opened the pit of the abyss; and there went up a smoke out of the pit, as the smoke of a great furnace; and the sun and the air were darkened by reason of the smoke of the pit" (verse two).

John gives personality to this star by defining it with the term "he." This is another proof that this star is not a celestial mass. There is obviously a shaft entrance to this pit. As soon as the entrance is opened, smoke begins to pour out! Smoke comes from fire. So, there was a fire in the pit. When there is fire and smoke, there is heat; the smoke was as if it came from a huge furnace, so the pit must have been very hot.

"And out of the smoke came forth locusts upon the earth; and power was given them, as the scorpions of the earth have power" (verse three).

In context, a horde of locusts came pouring out of the smoke of the pit. Locusts are a symbol of destruction. In the Old Testament, we see many instances where plagues of locusts destroyed vegetation, particularly when the Hebrews were leaving Egypt. During the time of these plagues, locusts ate all of the green vegetation of the entire country.

In addition to their ravenous appetites, these locusts were given the ability to sting like scorpions.

"And it was said unto them that they should not hurt the grass of the earth, neither any green thing, neither any tree, but only such men as have not the seal of God on their foreheads" (verse four).

The star came with instructions for these demonic bugs. These locusts were under God's orders to leave the earth's vegetation alone. Neither were they to harm anyone who had God's mark on their foreheads. They were sent for one purpose: to inflict pain on unbelievers!

Back in Revelation 7:1–3, you will recall, the angels who were holding the four winds in check were commanded: "Hurt not the earth, neither the sea, nor the trees, till we have sealed the servants of our God in their foreheads." Then follows the sealing of the 144,000. Here we get a little more information about the 144,000 who were sealed. They now have God's protective seal on their foreheads. They will not be affected in any way by the plagues that will fall on mankind.

"And it was given them that they should not kill them, but that they should be tormented five months: and their torment was as the torment of a scorpion, when it striketh a man" (verse five).

Though these "locusts" had the ability to sting, they were under orders not to sting people so badly that they would die. Their job was to torment them. It is said that the sting of the scorpion is like a hot needle sticking you and that the pain lasts for at least twenty-four hours and that then the pain will gradually disappear.

So, after the pain had diminished, the locusts would sting them again. This would continue for five months. Can you even imagine the pain? A bee sting hurts like crazy, and imagine the pain of the sting of a scorpion going on, and on, and on.

"And in those days men shall seek death, and shall in no wise find it; and they shall desire to die, and death fleeth from them" (verse six).

The pain of these stings will be so bad that men will try to commit suicide but will be unable to even kill themselves to be free from this agony. Talk about God's wrath! And this is just the beginning; there is much more to come.

"And the shapes of the locusts were like unto horses prepared for war; and upon their heads as it were crowns like unto gold, and their faces were as men's faces" (verse seven).

Now John sees locusts, and they are nothing like anyone has ever seen before! He has a hard time describing them. It would be like my grandmother trying to describe a microwave oven, a television set, or even an automobile or a plane. None of these were around during her lifetime. Nor have there been any bugs like these before.

So, John does what anyone would do: he compares them with something he knew about. As he describes these things, he uses the words "like" and "as if." "Like" denotes similarity in form or appearance. "As if" may express resemblance, but it also may describe the nature or action.

The detailed resemblances are given in order to enable the reader to get some idea of what they look like.

The description begins at the head and moves to the back. First, they have the appearance of a horse ready to be ridden into battle; that is: they have some type of armor on them. In England, I had the opportunity to go to the Tower of London and saw a room filled with armor. There were many suits of armor, including belonging to King Henry VIII. King Henry's horse's armor was there also. This armor covered the horse's head except for the ears and eyes. There was a breastplate for the chest and armor hanging down to protect the horse's flanks. All in all, quite impressive.

If you can picture a horse in armor, maybe you can get an idea of what John was trying to describe.

Next, John tells us that these creatures appeared to be wearing crowns, "like" crowns of gold. He doesn't say that they had the crowns on their heads, but it looks as if they did.

And they had faces "like" a man. We can imagine a lot of things here: eyes, nose, mouth. But whatever they look like or act like, they are definitely demonic.

"And they had hair as the hair of women, and their teeth were as teeth of lions" (verse eight).

John continues on with his description: they had long silky hair and sharp pointed teeth.

"And they had breastplates, as it were breastplates of iron; and the sound of their wings was as the sound of chariots, of many horses rushing to war" (verse nine).

Once again, I defer to my former statement about King Henry's horse's armor. These creatures, when flying, made a fearful noise. The noise was like that of the sound of an ancient battle, which had cavalry and charioteers in a huge breakneck charge. Clanging and banging of weapons, armor, yells, and the roar of chariot wheels. Can you imagine the terror produced by this horde of demonic bugs coming at you in a headlong charge?

I have never been in a battle, but those I know who have all say that the noise of the battle is horrible. In modern warfare, though, you can fight back. You can return fire against the enemy. Here, people won't be able to shoot the locusts. They will cover the land like hordes of locusts we see in ancient biblical times.

"And they have tails like unto scorpions, and stings; and in their tails is their power to hurt men for five months" (verse ten).

As in verse five of chapter nine, we see here the stings will continue for five months, continually causing great pain and despair.

"They have over them as king the angel of the abyss: his name in Hebrew is Abaddon, and in the Greek tongue he had the name Apollyon" (verse eleven).

Proverbs 30:27 says that "locusts have no king." These "locusts" differ from ordinary locusts in that they have a king over them. He has a name: *Abaddon* in the Hebrew language and *Apollyon* in Greek. Both names, in both languages, mean "destroyer" and appear no place else in the Bible.

This "destroyer" is a personality never before known. He is called the "angel of the abyss." Since he was in the abyss with the creatures, he would have to be one of the fallen angels who are the only other creatures that the Bible says are in the abyss.

"Abyss" is often translated as "bottomless pit." This "abyss" is the place where God confined the sinning angels who followed Lucifer in his rebellion against God and left their positions of authority in heaven. These will remain there, confined with bonds, until the final judgment.

This "angel," however, has been given the position of king over these "locusts." He will direct the creatures in their assault on those who live on the earth during the Tribulation period.

"The first Woe is past: behold, there come yet two Woes hereafter" (verse twelve).

As if that were not enough, John now tells us that there are two more woes to come! The indication here is that worse things are to follow. Remember, as the Tribulation period proceeds, things will get worse and worse.

And the sixth angel sounded, and I heard a voice from the horns of the golden altar which is before

God, one saying to the sixth angel that had one trumpet, Loose the four angels that are bound at the great river Euphrates.

Verses thirteen to fourteen

The sixth angel blows his trumpet and receives, in turn, orders from a voice emanating from the horns of the golden altar. He is now to turn loose the four angels who had been kept in abeyance at the Euphrates River. Why they were held at the Euphrates is not stated. This trumpet judgment will cover a greater amount of detail than any other. It includes the rest of this chapter, all of chapter ten, and as far as verse fourteen of chapter eleven.

Those involved, humans and spirit beings, are the most varied in nature and function in any of the judgments.

"And the four angels were loosed, that had been prepared for the hour and day and month and year, that they should kill the third part of men" (verse fifteen).

These four angels are not the angels from chapter seven. The angels in chapter seven are holy angels who are preserving and protecting nature, while the angels here are being set loose to kill men. Notice that they have been "bound." No holy angel would be bound! These are wicked, fallen angels who were cast out of heaven with Satan. And though wicked, these fallen angels are under the providence of God. They have been specially prepared for a specific time, down to the year, month, day, and hour, which was predetermined by God, in which they would carry out their specific purpose: that of destroying one-third of the population of the earth. When they are finished, the world population will have been reduced by another 25 percent. Remember, the population was reduced by 25 percent in chapter six, verse eight, by the rider of the pale horse. The resultant population is now reduced to half of the original.

"And the number of the armies of the horsemen was twice ten thousand times ten thousand: I heard the number of them" (verse sixteen).

Evidently, these four angels will be leading a demonic army, for here we are told that there is an army of "horsemen" that totals 200 million. To make sure that number was not misunderstood, John adds, "I heard the number!"

> And thus I saw the horses in the vision, and them that sat on them, having breastplates as of fire and of hyacinth and of brimstone: and the heads of lions; and out of their mouths proceedeth fire and smoke and brimstone.
>
> Verse seventeen

John now sees some very unusual "horses." These horses have riders. This is a demonic cavalry headed by the four fallen angels. The horses wear brightly colored breastplates of fiery red, dark blue, and dirty yellow. They have heads like a lion, and out of the horses' mouths come fire, smoke, and brimstone, or burning sulfur.

"By these three plagues was the third part of men killed, by the fire and the smoke of the and the brimstone, which proceeded out of their mouths" (verse eighteen).

It is by the plagues from these horses' mouths that one-third of mankind is killed. Notice: the fire is literal fire. The smoke is literal smoke. Added to the fact that already one-third of the sun's brightness has been diminished, this smoke will increase the darkness over the earth. The brimstone is reminiscent of the destruction of Sodom and Gomorrah.

"For the power of the horses is in their mouth, and in their tails: for their tails are like unto the serpents, and have heads; and with them they hurt" (verse nineteen).

One of the most unusual features of these "horses" is that they get you coming and going! If they miss you with fire, smoke, and brimstone from their mouths, they will get you with their tails that are not hair but poisonous snakes.

> And the rest of mankind, who were not killed with these plagues, repented not of the works of their hands, that they should not worship demons, and the idols of gold, and of silver, and of brass, and of stone, and of wood; which can neither see, nor hear, nor walk.
>
> Verse twenty

With half of the population of the earth gone, those left still would not repent! Isn't that amazing? You would think that after the combination of five months of torment and then death by fire, smoke, and brimstone, they would be on their knees and repent, but this is not to be. They have already admitted that this is the great wrath of God, yet they refuse to give up their lifestyle. They still continue to worship in false religions and make gods of their finances: money, investments, real estate, and other worthless possessions, which cause men to reject God.

"And they repented not of their murders, nor of their sorceries, nor of their fornication, nor of their thefts" (verse twenty-one).

Demon worship goes hand in hand with idolatry and will be the primary sin. Satan will want to be worshipped, and a great deal of perverted religion will be practiced. Added to this: demonic corruption leads to inhuman acts by those who reject God. These are listed as murderers, sorceries, and thefts.

> **Murderers.** Perversion of religious life leads to the perversion of social life. In this time, vices will have taken the place of virtues, and human life will have become cheap. We can already see that in some countries around the world where children are sold into slavery, and adults are killed for looking at someone the wrong way.
>
> **Sorceries.** The Greek word translated here as "sorceries" is pharmakeion, from which we get our English word, "pharmacy." Pharmacy means drugs. After the rapture of the church, drugs will play a large part in the lives of the unsaved.
>
> For instance, after being stung by the "locusts," people will try anything and everything to find something to deaden the pain. Although they will not die, they will feel as though they are dying.
>
> Drugs will be a part of religion. Just look at society today. Many people use alcohol, tobacco, a wide range of drugs, marijuana, opium, and many others I don't know about to numb their minds. With pushers encouraging people to be involved in reckless unrestricted usage,

many will become brain-dead. Still, those selling the drugs will do so with their consciences seared.

Sexual immorality. We have already seen the forerunner of the sexual revolution that will come. Remember the advertisement that said, "If it feels good, do it"? Well, without the restraining of the Holy Spirit on the earth and with society completely disintegrated, people will engage in sexual practices we have never heard of or want to hear of. Rape will be the order of the day. Homosexuality will then really be the alternate lifestyle. Pedophilia will not even cause an eye to blink. It will be much worse than Sodom and Gomorrah.

Thefts. Mankind will go back to the times of cavemen. It will be a society of "to the strong goes everything." If someone has something someone else wants, they will take it by hook, crook, or murder.

Add to this what we have already seen: if you have your bread ration, and someone else wants it, they will take it, even if they have to kill you and your family to get it.

This will be a time of complete lawlessness, with a man doing what is right in his own eyes (Judges 21:25). Things do not look too good for those on the earth, but God will still give the opportunity to repent.

This ends chapter nine, but there is still another woe to come. The worse is still to be revealed!

Chapter Ten

"And I saw another strong angel coming down out of heaven, arrayed with a cloud; and the rainbow was upon his head, and his face was as the sun, and his feet as pillars of fire" (verse one).

This vision is the longest in the book of Revelation. It covers three entire chapters (ten to twelve). John does not say, "I saw," again until chapter thirteen. We will see three major themes in these three chapters: the strong angel with the little book, the measuring of the Temple, and the martyrdom of the two witnesses.

There was a mighty angel referred to in chapter five, and now John writes of another strong angel who comes down out of heaven. This angel is said to be another angel of the same kind (Greek: *allon*). This one is described as having a reflection of the glory of God on his person. This description of the angel is like the brilliant light John saw when he was first taken to heaven and saw the throne of God.

Many commentators have tried to identify this person as Jesus Christ since He is described in an almost identical way, but in the book of Revelation, angels are always angels. Since I believe that we should interpret the Bible literally, I won't give this any more thought. This "strong angel" is definitely a personal representative of God Himself, but no further information is given concerning him.

"And he had in his hand a little book open: and he set his right foot upon the sea, and his left upon the earth" (verse two).

This angel carries a little scroll. It contains the rest of the prophetic message that John will record. Of significance is that this little scroll is open! Why would this be mentioned? Is there a connection with something that has been previously revealed? I think so!

If we go back to the book of Daniel, we will see that Daniel was given a vision of "Seventy weeks [which] are determined upon thy [Daniel's] people" (Daniel 9:24, KJV). In this vision, Daniel saw what would come to pass in the *end times*. From the perspective of a man living in 554 BC, this vision made little sense to Daniel. This prophetic vision, however, has become a reality, except for the last seven years covered. This last seven-year period is called the Great Tribulation (Matthew 24:21).

Daniel records, in chapter seven, that he had a night vision and that he wrote the "sum of all matters." In chapter twelve, God instructed him to seal up the book, even to the time of the end. When we come to this place in the book of Revelation, we are at the time of the end.

Therefore, we will now see what Daniel had been revealed that had to be sealed and could not be shown until this time. The book is now open!

"One foot on land and the other foot on the sea" is a symbol that indicates that this is for the entire earth and its inhabitants.

"And he cried with a great voice, as a lion roareth: and when he cried, the seven thunders uttered their voices" (verse three).

The lionlike roar is a signal that he is about to attack, which frightens its prey. When this roar was emitted, "seven thunders" spoke. This is the first reference in the scripture to "thunders" speaking. Since this is a heavenly vision John is experiencing, I conclude that these "thunders" are another type of heavenly being that has not previously been identified. From the context, they have an attribute of a person, that is, they speak. What they are saying is intelligible.

Physical thunder is produced by layers of warm and cold air rapidly expanding gases along the path of the electrical discharge of lightning. The result can be quite noisy. In fact, a strong clap of thunder can shake a house. Therefore, these voices that John hears are quite loud.

"And when the seven thunders uttered their voices, I was about to write: and I heard a voice from heaven saying, Seal up the things which the seven thunders uttered, and write them not" (verse four).

When these beings spoke, John wanted to write down what they were saying, but before he could start, he was ordered by a voice from heaven to stop writing and seal up the content of their message.

This is the only place in the book of Revelation where something is sealed. At the end of this book, John writes, "And he saith unto me, Seal not up the words of the prophecy of this book; for the time is at hand" (Revelation 22:10), yet this particular message of the seven thunders John is not allowed to write down. They will remain a secret until, and if, God reveals them in heaven.

And the angel that I saw standing upon the sea and upon the earth lifted up his right hand to heaven, and sware by him that liveth for ever and ever, who created the heaven and the things that are therein, and the earth and the things that that are therein, and the sea and the things that are therein, that there shall be delay no longer.

Verses five to six

John now records this strong angel lifts up his right hand to heaven and takes an oath to God that there will be no more delay. From this point on, the end-time events will proceed without interruption. God has been delaying His judgment so that last sinners would have time to repent. Now, however, He will accelerate His judgment and accomplish His purpose.

"But in the days of the voice of the seventh angel, when he is about to sound, then is finished the mystery of God, according to the good tidings which he declared to his servants the prophets" (verse seven).

Now the seventh angel with the seventh trumpet comes on the scene. He is just about to blow his trumpet to finish the mystery of God according to what He had revealed to His prophets. The seventh trumpet will reveal the final judgments of the bowls of God's wrath and the final establishment of God's rule on the earth.

"And the voice which I heard from heaven, I heard it again speaking with me, and saying, Go, take the book which is open in the hand of the angel that standeth upon the sea and upon the earth" (verse eight).

Before the angel can sound his trumpet, John hears a voice from heaven telling him to take the little open book from the strong angel.

> And I went unto the angel, saying unto him that he should give me the little book. And he saith unto me, Take it, and eat it up; And it shall make thy belly bitter, but in thy mouth it shall be sweet is honey.
>
> Verse nine

The strong angel still stands with one foot on the land and the other on the sea, which shows that what is transpiring is taking place on the earth. John walks up to the angel and asks him to give over the little scroll. When handing it over to John, the strong angel commands him to eat the scroll. When he eats it, it will taste as sweet as honey, but when it settles in his stomach, it will be as bitter as gall.

"And I took the little book out of the angel's hand, and ate it up; and it was in my mouth sweet as honey: and when I had eaten it, my belly was made bitter" (verse ten).

When John eats the little scroll, it is exactly as the strong angel describes: in his mouth, the scroll tastes like honey, but in his stomach, it turns bitter. Receiving the Word of God is a great joy, but since this little scroll proclaims a message of more wrath and woe, it results in an unpleasant experience. In any case, the sweetness should not be taken to refer to the joy of proclaiming a message of wrath, for to all God's prophets, this was a sorrowful task. But the commission to write these words, which are to the nation of Israel, sits heavy on the stomach.

"And they say unto me, Thou must prophesy again over many peoples and nations and tongues and kings" (verse eleven).

Another thing that doesn't sit well with John is the fact that he must prophesy to the whole world before Christ comes back to set up His kingdom. This prophecy is against all those who will be living on the earth at this time: every race (peoples), every country (nations), and every ruler (kings). There is more judgment to come after this. Please remember we are still in the middle of the Tribulation at this point.

Like John, we Christians must devour and digest the content of this book and carry a warning to our lost world concerning future events. To those who reject this message because of disbelief, the message will be forever bitter and bring agony and fear. To those who listen to this message and come to Christ, the message will be eternally sweet.

This concludes chapter ten.

Chapter Eleven

"And there was given me a reed like unto a rod: and one said, Rise, and measure the temple of God, and the altar, and them that worship therein" (verse one).

The reed is a species of cane that grows in abundance in the Jordan River valley and grows as high as twenty feet. Being both light and durable, reeds were used in various ways, one of which was as measuring sticks, or rods. We can see an example of a measuring rod in Ezekiel 40:5, where the length is said to be "six cubits long." Since a cubit is approximately eighteen inches, a typical rod would be six by eighteen, or nine feet long.

The purpose of the reed is to measure the Temple of God and the altar. John was also to count (measure) the worshippers who were in the Temple.

"And the court which is without the temple leave without, and measure it not; for it hath been given unto the nations: and the holy city shall they tread under foot forty and two months" (verse two).

From this verse, it appears that the Temple proper, the altar of incense, and the Holy of Holies, and those who are within worshipping, are to be secured for God in view of the defilement that is to be inflicted soon. The Greek word for the Temple proper is hieron, while the Greek word used here is naos and refers to the inner court only. The outer court is not to be included in the measurement, for it will be given over to the "nations" (Gentiles), or unbelievers, who are primarily non-Jews, for a period of forty-two months. I say *primarily* because many unbelievers will be Jews. And once again, I remind you that the time now is mid-Tribulation, for forty-two months is three and a half years. This is the beginning of the second half of the Tribulation period.

"And I will give unto my two witnesses, and they shall prophesy a thousand two hundred and threescore days, clothed in sackcloth" (verse three).

We see that there will be two witnesses for God coming on the scene. They will prophesy for 1,260 days; 1,260 days is forty-two of the Jewish months of thirty days each, or three and a half years. We will see when they will be witnessing in verse seven.

In some translations, it reads that God will give the power to His two witnesses. The word "power" is not in the Greek text! What God will give them are the words to say.

"Clothed in sackcloth" suggests that these two witnesses will be preaching a message of repentance, such as in Isaiah 37:1–2. Many have tried to name these two witnesses, and most named them Elijah and Moses. But good intentions should never be reasons to put words in God's mouth. If the Scriptures do not give you the information, say so! We do not have their names.

"These are the two olive trees and the two candlesticks, standing before the Lord of the earth" (verse four).

They are also called "olive trees" and "candlesticks." Olive trees give oil for the lamps, and candlesticks are light bearers.

Therefore, their mission is to expose the light of God in a dark, dark world. We see these same two "olive trees" in Zechariah 4:11–14, where they are defined as "the two anointed ones, that stand by the Lord of the whole earth" (Zechariah 4:14). Here in the book of Revelation, John uses the same verbiage. Standing before the Lord denotes service or worship. Here it means to serve God.

"And if any man desireth to hurt them [these two], fire proceedeth out of their mouth and devoureth their enemies; and if any man shall desire to hurt them, in this manner must he be killed" (verse five).

If anyone even has the desire to hurt them, he or she will be instantly destroyed by the fire issuing from their mouths. This is a commandment from God. We are talking about fire hot enough to burn them to cinders immediately!

> These have the power to shut the heaven, that it rain not during the days of their prophecy: and they have the power over the waters to turn them into blood, and to smite the earth with every plague, as often as they shall desire.
>
> Verse six

These two witnesses are given unlimited authority. They can control rainfall, and they are able to turn water into blood. They can bring on any plague they desire, and they can do these things whenever they wish.

"And when they shall have finished their testimony, the beast that cometh up out of the abyss shall make war with them, and overcome them, and kill them" (verse seven).

Now we find out that these two witnesses will be ministering: they complete their testimony, and when they are completely finished, the beast that comes up out of the abyss will war against them. He will defeat them and kill them.

This is the first reference to the beast in the book of Revelation. We will see more of this beast in the rest of the book.

"And their dead bodies lie in the street of the great city, which spiritually is called Sodom and Egypt, where also their Lord was crucified" (verse eight).

These men will not be given a decent burial. In Israel, when a person dies, they must be buried the same day, before nightfall. The Greek word translated into English as "dead bodies" is actually potoma, which is properly translated as "carcasses." This denotes the contempt and hatred the world will have for the two witnesses. They are treated like dead animals or, like we say, roadkill.

The city is, of course, Jerusalem.

"And from among the peoples and tribes and tongues and nations do men look upon their dead bodies three days and a half, and suffer not their dead bodies to be laid in a tomb" (verse nine).

People from all around the world will either come to Jerusalem or watch on television the dead bodies lying in the street. With morbid curiosity, they will relish the opportunity to gaze at the dead men. They will lay in the heat of the day, flies buzzing around them, and whatever other things happen to untended corpses will take place, and no one will lift a hand to give them decent burials.

This for a Jew is unthinkable!

"And they that dwell on the earth rejoice over them, and make merry; and they shall send gifts to one another; because these two prophets tormented them that dwell on the earth" (verse ten).

Their deaths will be an opportunity to celebrate. The witnesses who have pointed out their sin natures will have finally been silenced, and people will not have them pointing the finger at them anymore. They will be able to carry on their wicked ways now that these two will not be around to chastise them for it. It will be a big worldwide party with people sending presents. This will be the devil's Christmas party! All will gloat over their deaths.

Then something happens:

"And after three days and a half the breath of life from God entered into them, and they stood up on their feet; and great fear fell upon them that beheld them" (verse eleven).

While the world is partying and celebrating the deaths of these two witnesses, and while the whole world is watching, the two witnesses will be touched by God. They will begin to breathe; their color will return; their rotten bodies will be restored; they will be completely regenerated, and they will stand on their feet.

The television media will regret they had coverage of their resurrection because they will not want to give this news. While any news like this would be a scoop for the media, it will stand as a battle lost for the devil.

At their resurrection and reappearing, great fear will come over the unsaved. This will separate believers from unbelievers.

There is some significance in the bodies lying in the street for three and a half days. The ancient Israelites believed that a person could come back to life within three days, but longer than that, they were definitely dead.

"And they heard a great voice from heaven saying unto them, Come up hither. And they went up into heaven in the cloud; and their enemies beheld them" (verse twelve).

Not only are the two witnesses miraculously raised from the dead, but they are then caught up to heaven. God rescues them from their enemies and gives witness to the whole world.

The world's great joy now turns to great fear.

> And in that hour there was a great earthquake, and the tenth part of the city fell; and there were killed in the earthquake seven thousand persons: and the rest were affrighted, and gave glory to the God of heaven.
>
> Verse thirteen

Their fear will increase when a huge earthquake takes place, killing 7,000 men and destroying one-tenth of Jerusalem. There was a great earthquake when the sixth seal was opened. This one is much worse. The earthquake is a further sign of God's vindication of His servants, but unlike the one in the sixth seal, this produces what appears to be repentance, for the survivors "gave glory to God."

However, their supposed repentance comes from their fear. They know that everything happening around them is supernatural, and they have to admit that God is in charge. They have to give God the glory, for He is the only One who can bring such judgment.

In addition to this, we still have the rest of the Tribulation to consider, and there are still many people left in Jerusalem who are unsaved.

"The second Woe is past: behold, the third Woe cometh quickly" (verse fourteen).

As we have seen, the *first* woe was in Revelation 9:2–12; the *second* in Revelation 9:13–11:13; And now comes the *third* woe. The seventh trumpet is now ready to sound.

> And the seventh angel sounded; and there followed great voices in heaven, and they said, The kingdom of the world is become the kingdom of our Lord, and of his Christ: and he shall reign for ever and ever.
>
> Verse fifteen

Back in Revelation 10:7, this verse, "In the days of the seventh angel, when he shall sound, the mystery of God is finished" (paraphrased), implies that everything from here on is contained in the seventh trumpet and will take history to the end of the Tribulation period, and the end of God's wrath.

And now we see an interlude that takes place in heaven. The seventh trumpet sounds, and we hear "great voices in heaven." The text doesn't say how many in this instance, only that they were very loud. Neither does it say who the voices belong to. But it does say that they were sounding. Their chant praises God for the completion of His plan for mankind. The earth will now be given over to Jesus Christ by God the Father, and when this final trumpet judgment has been completed, Jesus will set up His kingdom where He will reign eternally.

And the four and twenty elders, who sit before God on
their thrones, fell upon their faces and worshipped
God, saying, We give thee thanks, O Lord God, the
Almighty, who art and who wast; because thou has
taken thy great power, and didst reign.

Verses sixteen to seventeen

We see the twenty-four elders again. This time they are
seated on their thrones. When they hear the chant of the loud
voices around them, they get off their thrones, prostrate themselves, and facedown, worship God and give Him thanks. Their
thanks include the fact that God is the only God, He existed
in eternity, He died on the cross, He was resurrected, and will
now take His throne.

And the nations were wroth, and thy wrath came, and
the time of the dead to be judged, and the time to give
their reward to thy servants the prophets, and to the
saints, and to them that fear thy name, the small and
the great; and to destroy them that destroy the earth.

Verse eighteen

The twenty-four elders continue their praise of God with
events that will be taking place in the remainder of the chapters of the book of Revelation. They list the events: the nations
of the earth were very angry at God; God's wrath has come; the
time for judging the wicked dead is present, and it is time for
God's prophets, servants, and saints, and all those who stood in

awe of God, the small and great, to be given their rewards for their faithfulness. But it is also time to destroy those who have destroyed the earth.

"And there was opened the temple of God that is in heaven; and there was seen in his temple the ark of his covenant" (verse nineteen).

In the Old Testament tabernacle and Temple, no one was permitted in the Holy of Holies where the ark was kept except the high priest. The high priest was allowed to enter one day in the year, the day of atonement. On this day, he would sprinkle blood on the mercy seat to cover the sins of Israel for the year.

But now, we see no veil in the Temple of God. We see everything out in the open. We need no high priest to intercede for us. Our King Jesus has made us a race of priests, and we have access to His Temple without impediment. The Ark of the Covenant is there for all to see. This ark led Israel through the Jordan River and into their inheritance. This vision would encourage God's people to whom John would send this book. God will fulfill His promises.

The ark reminds them of His presence and the faithfulness of His promises.

"And there followed lightnings, and voices, and thunders, and an earthquake, and great hail" (verse nineteen, part b).

With each scene that is presented to John, the wrath of God increases in intensity. It marks the close of events of great importance and transitions into more of the wrath to come. We see this now as there is sharp lightning, many voices gathered together in heaven, rolling thunder of intense magnitude, earthquakes one after another, and huge hailstones. In context, we are not told how big these hailstones are in size.

In my lifetime, I have seen a good deal of hail. Normal hailstones range in size from BB size to the size of a golf ball. In recent years, hailstones have increased in size, and reports of hail the size of softballs and larger have become almost ordinary. We will come to another reference about the size of hailstones in Revelation 16:21, where it says the stones are about the weight of a talent. We are talking about some huge chunks of ice falling from the sky since a talent is about a hundred pounds.

So, regardless of actual size, these hailstones will put some dings in cars, for they will be of unusual size. More of this when we get to chapter sixteen.

Chapter Twelve

"And a great sign was seen in heaven: a woman arrayed with the sun, and the moon under her feet, and upon her head a crown of twelve stars" (verse one).

John now sees a sign in heaven. It is a special sign to John. For those of you who used the King James Version of the Bible, your Bible reads, "A great wonder appeared." The Greek word for "wonder" is *teras*. The Greek word used here is *sameion* and means "a sign." *Teras* is not used in the book of Revelation! *Sameion* is used sixteen times in the New Testament and is always translated as a "sign."

A sign is a visible picture given to the observer, by which it can be understood. Therefore, in this vision, John is able to get the message quickly.

He sees a woman clothed with the sun, and she stands on the moon. She has a crown on her head composed of twelve stars. In particular, this woman's identity is in her clothing. She is clothed with the sun. She is standing on the moon, and she has a crown that is composed of twelve stars.

In searching Scripture for similar or like passages, we come to Genesis 37:9–10. The resemblance is very much like the picture we see here, and the implications are nearly identical. If you recall, Joseph was sold into slavery by his eleven brothers, and the rejected brother (Joseph) had a dream in which the sun, the moon, and the eleven stars bowed down before him. He told his dream to his father and his brothers and, in his reply, his father asked Joseph, "Shall I, your mother, and your brothers bow down ourselves to you on the earth?" (Genesis 37:10, paraphrased).

The ultimate symbolism is clear: the woman stands for Israel. She is clothed in the glory of God. Isaiah 60:1–3, 20 (KJV) says to the nation of Israel,

> Arise, shine; for thy light is come, and the glory of the LORD is risen upon thee. For, behold, the darkness shall cover the earth, and gross darkness the people: but the LORD shall arise upon thee, and his glory shall be seen upon thee. And the Gentiles shall come to thy light, and kings to the brightness of that thy rising. [...] Thy sun shall no more go down; neither shall thy moon withdraw itself: for the LORD shall be thine everlasting light, and the days of thy mourning shall be ended.

So, not only are the Israelites God's chosen people, Israel is clothed in God's glory, and God's glory will never leave Israel again.

The twelve stars are representative of the twelve tribes that are restored in Israel during the Tribulation period after some two thousand years (if Jesus would come this year).

"And she was with child; and she crieth out, travailing in birth, and in pain to be delivered" (verse two).

Compare this verse with a prophetic message from Old Testament.

> But thou, Bethlehem Ephratah, though thou be little among the thousands of Judah, yet out of thee shall he come forth unto me that is to be ruler in Israel; whose goings forth have been from of old, from everlasting. Therefore will he give them up, until the time that she which travaileth hath brought forth: then the remnant of his brethren shall return unto the children of Israel.
>
> Micah 5:2–3 (KJV)

First, Micah prophesies that the "ruler of Israel" will come out of Bethlehem. This "ruler" will also come from eternity and will have been in existence and in action throughout all of the time. This "ruler" will give up on Israel until the time when she will "travail."

The context indicates that Israel will be under attack continuously because of its position of favor with God. Additionally, Israel is the nation from which the King of kings would be born, who would defeat the dragon whom we see in the next verse.

"And there was seen another sign in heaven: and behold, a great red dragon, having seven heads and ten horns, and upon his head seven diadems" (verse three).

John now sees another sign in heaven. This time he sees an individual, "a great red dragon." The sign is not just that a dragon appears, but that it is *a great red dragon*. Red is the color of blood and denotes his murderous purpose. Scriptures say he was a "murderer from the beginning" (John 8:44); he is called this now because of the emphasis on the end times and the warfare and destruction that will take place as he tries to destroy Israel.

The name "dragon" is used throughout the Old Testament to describe a particular adversary of Israel. We will see this person identified in verse nine of this chapter, but for now, we will look at him as the great red dragon and withhold his identification.

Not only does John see a dragon, but this dragon has seven heads, ten horns, and ten crowns. These features add to the identification of the dragon.

Working in reverse, ten diadems, or crowns, indicate that this dragon has, under his control, ten kingdoms. We must refer to the book of Daniel to see how this will come about:

> The fourth beast shall be the fourth kingdom upon earth, which shall be diverse from all kingdoms, and shall devour the whole earth, and shall tread it down, and break it in pieces. And the ten horns out of this kingdom are ten kings that shall arise: and another shall rise after them; and he shall be diverse from the first, and he shall subdue three kings. And he shall speak great words against the most High, and shall wear out the saints of the most High, and think to change times and laws: and they shall be given into his hand until a time and times and the dividing of time.
>
> Daniel 7:23–25 (KJV)

In context, this very unusual-looking dragon will be the fourth of four kingdoms described in Daniel, chapter seven. When we read this chapter, we see that Daniel was in captivity in Babylon.

To understand all of this, we will now have to do a study of Daniel, chapter seven:

"In the first year of Belshazzar king of Babylon Daniel had a dream and visions of his head upon his bed: then he wrote the dream, and told the sum of the matters" (Daniel 7:1).

Nebuchadnezzar had died, and Belshazzar assumed his throne. In the first year of Belshazzar's reign, Daniel, who was in Babylonian captivity, had a dream. It sounds more like a nightmare, but Scripture calls it a dream.

Daniel recorded everything he saw in his dream. He tells us about it in chapter seven.

"Daniel spake and said, I saw in my vision by night, and, behold, the four winds of the heaven strove upon the great sea" (Daniel 7:2).

Daniel tells us now what he saw: first, his vision was a night vision. When this vision began, Daniel saw the "four winds of heaven," and they exerted a great deal of energy on the sea.

"And four great beasts came up from the sea, diverse one from another" (Daniel 7:3).

Their winds churned up the sea, and when this happened, four great beasts came up out of the sea.

Daniel is perturbed and seeks an explanation. In response, God informs him that the four beasts represent four earthly kings who would be worldwide rulers. They came out of mankind (the sea), and each of them is totally different from another.

The first was like a lion, and had eagle's wings: I beheld till the wings thereof were plucked, and it was
lifted up from the earth, and made to stand upon the
feet as a man, and a man's heart was given to it.

Daniel 7:4

At a later time in Daniel's life, he has a vision where he is giv-
en the identity of these four kings. In Daniel, chapter eight, the
prophet identifies this first beast as Nebuchadnezzar, the king
of Babylon. The image of the lion's wings that were plucked off
speaks of him being removed from his throne and having to live
in the fields and live like an animal. Later, when he repented of
his sins, God restored him to his throne.

And behold another beast, a second, like to a bear,
and it raised up itself on one side, and it had three
ribs in the mouth of it between the teeth of it: and
they said thus unto it, Arise, devour much flesh.

Daniel 7:5 (KJV)

The second beast is identified as Cyrus, the king of Medo-
Persia. Cyrus became the second worldwide ruler when he con-
quered the Lydian Empire of Asia Minor, the Chaldean Empire,
and the Kingdom of Egypt. These three kingdoms are the three
ribs in the bear's mouth. Being "raised up on one side" means
that the Median Empire would dominate the Persian Empire,
although joined together. This empire would go on to dominate
and "devour" the rest of the world.

"After this I beheld, and lo another, like a leopard, which had upon the back of it four wings of a fowl; the beast had also four heads; and dominion was given to it" (Daniel 7:6, KJV).

The third beast that Daniel saw was Alexander the Great, king of Greece. This beast, the leopard, represents Alexander's swiftly moving army, who soon defeated the Medo-Persians and became the fourth worldwide leader. The four wings and the four heads represent Alexander's four generals, Lysimachus, Seleucus, Antipater, Ptolemy.

After Alexander's death, these four generals would assume control over Alexander's domain. However, the Scriptures say, none of these four would ever rule over the entire world. Daniel 8:22 confirms this.

> After this I saw in the night visions, and behold a fourth beast, dreadful and terrible, and strong exceedingly; and it had great iron teeth: it devoured and brake in pieces, and stamped the residue with the feet of it: and it was diverse from all the beasts that were before it; and it had ten horns.
>
> Daniel 7:7 (KJV)

Now Daniel sees a fourth beast who is not identified because he is totally different from the three who came before him or is known to history. This empire will be even fiercer and stronger than the three that precede him. The "teeth of iron" mean that he will have more crushing power, exploitation, and repression than the other three and that what he cannot control or kill, he will trample underfoot.

One major way that this beast differs from the three who will precede him is that he will have "ten horns."

> I considered the horns, and, behold, there came among them another little horn, before whom there were three of the first horns plucked up by the roots: and, behold, in this horn were eyes like the eyes of man, and a mouth speaking great things.
>
> Daniel 7:8 (KJV)

Daniel was puzzled by these ten horns. What did they mean? There is a definite correspondence between these ten horns and the ten toes of iron and Nebuchadnezzar's dream in chapter two.

> This is the dream; and we will tell the interpretation thereof before the king. Thou, O king, art a king of kings: for the God of heaven hath given thee a kingdom, power, and strength, and glory. And wheresoever the children of men dwell, the beasts of the field and the fowls of the heaven hath he given into thine hand, and hath made thee ruler over them all. Thou art this head of gold. And after thee shall arise another kingdom inferior to thee, and another third kingdom of brass, which shall bear rule over all the earth. And the fourth kingdom shall be strong as iron: forasmuch as iron breaketh in pieces and subdueth all things: and as iron that breaketh all these, shall it break in pieces and bruise. And whereas thou

sawest the feet and toes, part of potters' clay, and part of iron, the kingdom shall be divided; but there shall be in it of the strength of the iron, forasmuch as thou sawest the iron mixed with miry clay. And as the toes of the feet were part of iron, and part of clay, so the kingdom shall be partly strong, and partly broken. And whereas thou sawest iron mixed with miry clay, they shall mingle themselves with the seed of men: but they shall not cleave to one another, even as iron is not mixed with clay. And in the days of these kings shall the God of heaven set up a kingdom, which shall never be destroyed: and the kingdom shall not be left to other people, but it shall break in pieces and consume all these kingdoms, and it shall stand forever. Forasmuch as thou sawest that the stone was cut out of the mountain without hands, and that it brake into pieces the iron, the brass, the clay, the silver, and the gold; the great God hath made known to the king what shall come to pass hereafter: and the dream is certain, and the interpretation thereof sure.

Daniel 2:36–45 (KJV)

Daniel saw four kings in Nebuchadnezzar's dream. The fourth king would rule over the fourth kingdom. As he considered what these kings stood for, he saw someone come out of one of ten kingdoms on the earth, defeat, or take over three of the kingdoms, and set himself up as ruler of the other seven.

This description implies that this little horn has a mouth that speaks boastfully and hints at this ruler as arrogant and glorifying himself. He will promote himself worldwide.

Therefore, the seven heads are seven kingdoms. The beast has these seven heads on himself, which indicates that he is ruling over all ten nations, and he is wearing all ten crowns.

Now, back to chapter twelve of Revelation.

We go back to John's vision now:

> And his tail draweth the third part of the stars of heaven, and did cast them to the earth: and the dragon standeth before the woman that is about to be delivered, that when she is delivered he may devour her child.
>
> Verse four

The red dragon, or Satan, had managed to persuade one-third of all of the heavenly beings to rebel against God. For his act of rebellion, Satan was expelled from heaven and sent to the earth, where he was given authority to rule. When he left heaven, those beings whom he caused to fall were drawn to the earth with him. We see Satan now standing before Israel, waiting for her to give birth to the Messiah. Satan would do anything in his power over men to destroy this child.

"And she was delivered of a son, a man child, who is to rule all the nations with a rod of iron: and her child was caught up unto God, and unto his throne" (verse five).

The woman, Israel, delivered a man child. This son of Israel will become the fifth world ruler.

We see in these two verses thousands of years of battle between Satan and God. In verse five, the dragon is ready to destroy the Messiah born of Israel, but He is taken away to His throne before the dragon can harm Him.

This woman will be doubly persecuted because Jesus will come from Israel, and the devil knows at this time that he is in deep trouble. Israel will be suffering during this time, and she will long for her Messiah to come and deliver her from her pain.

"And the woman fled into the wilderness, where she hath a place prepared of God, that there they may nourish her a thousand two hundred and threescore days" (verse six).

Here in verse six, we fast-forward to the Tribulation period, where the dragon tries to annihilate Israel. He knows that if Israel is destroyed, the Messiah's kingdom cannot come. But God miraculously protects her and leads the people to a pre-prepared place of safety where they will be cared for for the remainder of the Tribulation period (1,260 days, or three and a half years).

"And there was war in heaven: Michael and his angels going forth to war with the dragon; and the dragon warred and his angels" (verse seven).

Here in verse seven, we have a flashback to heaven. We see Michael, the archangel, whose ministry is to oversee and protect the nation of Israel. He is in a battle being fought against the devil and his demons.

"And they prevailed not, neither was their place found any more in heaven" (verse eight).

Michael gains the victory over the devil and casts him out of heaven once and for all, thereby excluding him from access to God.

And the great dragon was cast down, the old serpent, he that is called the Devil and Satan, the deceiver of the whole world; he was cast down to the earth, and his angels were cast down with him.

Verse nine

This is the first of three judgments against Satan. He will eventually be bound, sealed in a bottomless pit, and finally thrown into the eternal lake of fire. This battle will take place in the middle of the Tribulation period. This is supported by Scripture and Daniel 12:1, where Michael defends Israel during the Tribulation.

> And at that time shall Michael stand up, the great prince who standeth for the children of thy people; and there shall be a time of trouble, such as never was since there was a nation even to that same time: and at that time thy people shall be delivered, every one that shall be found written in the book.

Daniel 12:1

> And I heard a great voice in heaven, saying, Now is come the salvation, and the power, and the kingdom of our God, and the authority of his Christ: for the accuser of our brethren is cast down, who accuseth them before our God day and night.

Verse ten

The removal of the devil from heaven produces a victory cry. It is a cry of praise that is given to celebrate the completion of God's program. Satan is defeated! He is no longer allowed to stand before the throne of God, accusing the followers of Jesus Christ.

"And they overcame him because of the blood of the Lamb, and because of the word of their testimony; and they loved not their life even unto death" (verse eleven).

These followers of Jesus Christ, who come to Him during the Tribulation period, have overcome the devil because of their witness for Him. Through their testimony and the resultant salvation of those to whom they witness and who come to Christ, they have overcome the devil even though they lost their lives.

"Therefore rejoice, O heavens, and ye that dwell in them. Woe for the earth and for the sea: because of the devil is gone down unto you, having great wrath, knowing that he had but a short time" (verse twelve).

The world, already under the wrath of God, must now face the uncontrollable anger of the devil as he pours out irrational hatred on Israel, and thus all of humanity.

Why such intense hatred? He knows he only has a short amount of time left to accomplish his objectives before he is cast into the bottomless pit.

"And when the dragon saw that he was cast down to the earth, he persecuted the woman that brought forth the man child" (verse thirteen).

The devil now goes after Israel in earnest. These people are the ones who have been his death knell. His nemesis, Jesus, came for them, and the devil will do everything within his power to destroy them completely. He knows that if he can destroy them, he will put a crimp in God's program and keep it from coming to its final completion.

And there were given to the woman the two wings of
the great eagle, that she might fly into the wilderness
unto her place, where she is nourished for a time, and
times, and half a time, from the face of the serpent.

Verse fourteen

Israel will be miraculously taken to safety. The term "eagle's
wings" was used to describe Israel's flight from Egypt and
doesn't necessarily mean that Israel will be taken through the
air. Besides, the location of the "wilderness" is not given since
the place of refuge will be hidden from the devil. John says that
Israel will be fed and kept "for a time," "times," and "half a time."
The "time" is one year. Therefore, there are three times, and half
a time, which add up to three and a half years, which correlates
with the last three years of the Tribulation period.

"And the serpent cast out of his mouth after the woman water as a river, that he might cause her to be carried away by the
stream" (verse fifteen).

In an attempt to destroy Israel, Satan will cause a flood to
begin, which he thinks will destroy Israel by drowning her.

"And the earth helped the woman, and the earth opened her
mouth and swallowed up the river which the dragon cast out of
his mouth" (verse sixteen).

Israel will be spared from this flood when the earth opens
up to channel the water into the ground. In context, it appears
as though this is an earthquake that opens a fault line into
which the water flows. However it is done, Israel is safe from
drowning.

"And the dragon waxed wroth with the woman, and went away to make war with the rest of her seed, that keep the commandments of God, and hold the testimony of Jesus" (verse seventeen).

Being unable to destroy Israel will make the devil even angrier and will cause him to go after those Jews who are left behind. These are probably the 144,000 protected by God, and the devil will only become more frustrated when he is thwarted.

Although he will be unable to destroy Israel totally, the devil will exterminate two-thirds of the Jewish people during the Tribulation period.

Chapter Thirteen

"And he stood upon the sand of the sea. And I saw a beast coming up out of the sea, having ten horns, and seven heads, and on his horns ten diadems, and upon his heads names of blasphemy" (verse one).

The dragon stands on the sideline waiting for someone, and John sees a *beast* come out of the sea. This *beast* has ten horns and seven heads. He wears a crown on each of his ten horns. These ten horns are referred to in Daniel 7:7, in his vision of this fourth empire.

I have been trying not to solve the puzzle of the identity of the seven horns until we reach the scripture that provides the necessary information, but here I have to break my own rule and refer to a later chapter. A beast can only have one head at a time! The seven heads, therefore, are successive. We see this point in Revelation 17:9, where the seven heads are seven mountains, and in Revelation 17:10, we see these seven mountains are seven kings. Five are fallen; that is, they have died. One is, that is the one who is, who was living when John lived, and the other is yet to come.

Note carefully: the heads are said to be kings (or emperors); they are successive in order; the last mentioned has not yet come.

The identities of these kings are given to us in the history of Israel. These are the kings who held Israel in bondage. The first was in Egypt (1730 BC), then Assyria (722 BC), then Babylon (605 BC), then Medo-Persia (539 BC), and then Greece (336 BC). At the time this book was written, Rome had Israel in subjection.

That brings us to the next ruler who will take Israel into bondage, and that ruler will be this beast.

"And the beast which I saw was like unto a leopard" (verse two).

The leopard was a symbol of the Greek empire of Alexander the Great. Like the leopard, Alexander moved swiftly through the Middle East, destroying his "prey." This beast will have all of the swiftness in warfare of Alexander.

"And his feet were as the feet of a bear" (verse two, part b).

His feet being like that of a bear is a symbol of the Medo-Persian empire of Cyrus that speaks of stability, tenacity, and the strength to crush his enemy at will.

"And his mouth as the mouth of a lion" (verse two, part c).

His mouth "as the mouth of a lion" is a symbol of the Babylonian Empire under Nebuchadnezzar and speaks of majesty, power, and ferocity.

Therefore, this beast will have all of the characteristics of the three former world rulers.

"And the dragon gave him his power, and his throne, and great authority" (verse two, part d).

Then the dragon (*Satan*) gave this beast his power (that is, Satan's power); he relinquished his throne and gave to this beast unlimited authority to do as he would. So, although a pawn in the hands of Satan and controlled by him, this beast will possess greater authority and power than all these successive empires before him.

"And I saw one of his heads as though it had been smitten unto death; and his death-stroke was healed: and the whole earth wondered after the beast" (verse three).

The word for "wound" in the Greek text is plege, which, when properly translated, is "plague." This plague is a divinely inflicted judgment. In verse fourteen, it tells us that the beast was healed from a wound caused by a sword. This fatal blow has fallen on the great dragon as well. It was caused by Jesus' death, resurrection, and exultation. This blow is said to be the blow of a sword, which is the victor's weapon.

Since the beast came up out of the abyss, in John's description of him, we will see a number of parallels with Jesus that should be considered. His wound unto death counterfeits Jesus' death on the cross. His healed head counterfeits Jesus' resurrection, and his upcoming exultation counterfeits Jesus' return to heaven as King of kings. We will talk more about this counterfeit later.

"And they worshipped the dragon, because he gave his authority unto the beast; and they worshipped the beast, saying, Who is like unto the beast?" (verse four).

And here we see the beginning of open, unrestrained devil worship. This worship is, however, worship that is forced on mankind because of the power and the authority that Satan now has, with the church gone from the earth and the wrath of God being poured out on the earth's inhabitants.

Their worship is for the seventh ruler of the earth.

And who is able to war with him?

Who indeed! Not man. Man will not have the strength or ability to stand up against this representative of the devil, much less fight against him. Even Michael, one of the strongest heavenly beings, disputed with the devil over Moses's body and couldn't stand alone against him but had to tell him that the Lord rebuked him (Jude 9), and now the citizens of the earth have to contend with the devil and his representative, and with no help from the Holy Spirit.

"And there was given to him a mouth speaking great things and blasphemies; and there was given to him authority to continue forty and two months" (verse five).

Like most world dictators, the beast will be a persuasive speaker. He will be very charismatic and will be able to mesmerize people all around the world with his inspiring speeches. The devil gives the beast a big mouth! He goes around telling everyone how great he is and what great things he will do and, at the same time, will be cursing and damning God. God will allow the beast to do this, but He will limit him to forty-two months, or until the last half of the Tribulation period is ended. Then He will put a stop to the beast's big mouth!

"And he opened his mouth for blasphemies against God, to blaspheme his name, and his tabernacle, even them that dwell in the heaven" (verse six).

This verse lists three ways the beast will blaspheme against God: he will slander God; he will revive the temple, and he will speak contemptibly about those who have gone to heaven and to those who live in heaven: God, Jesus, the Holy Spirit, and all of the heavenly creation.

"And it was given unto him to make war with the saints, and overcome them: and there was given to him authority over every tribe and people and tongue and nation" (verse seven).

The beast will kill millions during the latter part of the Tribulation period. He will particularly seek out those who turn to God. These are the "saints" of whom John is speaking. A saint is one who has been *sanctified*, or set apart by God.

These saints will be those who accept Jesus as their Messiah during the Tribulation period.

The beast will be given the power to rule over the entire world population.

"And all that dwell on the earth shall worship him, every one whose name hath not been written from the foundation of the world in the book of life of the Lamb that hath been slain" (verse eight).

Those who do not have their names written in the Lamb's book of life will be the ones who will worship the beast and the devil. They will set him up as their god and forget about the one God of heaven.

"If any man hath an ear, let him hear" (verse nine).

John inserts a warning to everyone reading this book. He warns everyone that there will be a war against God's people and the beast's attempt to gain worldwide worship. It is a solemn warning with life-threatening consequences, but more than that, it is eternal life threatening.

"If any man is for captivity, into captivity he goeth: if any man shall kill with his sword, with the sword must he be killed. Here is the patience and the faith of the saints" (verse ten).

Divine judgment will be poured out on the beast and his followers who kill Tribulation saints. This also points out that

Tribulation saints will undergo severe persecution and martyrdom by the beast and his army. However, whatever they dish out will come back to them, and they will receive from God what they have done to His people. Therefore, the saints are warned of their coming martyrdom and urged to submit to the persecution; for a death, they will become victorious.

Even in this dismissal prophecy, there is a glimmer of hope. God is still in control and has limited this persecution to forty-two months.

"And I saw another beast coming out of the earth; and he had two horns like unto a lamb, and he spake as a dragon" (verse eleven).

Yet another *beast* appears on the scene. This one comes up out of the earth. The word "another" is *allos* in the Greek text. *Allos* means "another of the same kind." This beast will look different but will have the same characteristics as the first beast. He will seem to be like a lamb; that is, he will appear to be peaceful, but he will not speak peace. Instead, he will use the same language as the devil.

The "two horns" indicate that this is a male since female sheep have no horns. This denotes strength.

"And he exerciseth all the authority of the first beast in his sight. And he maketh the earth and them dwell therein to worship the first beast, whose death-stroke was healed" (verse twelve).

In his lamblike appearance, he will seductively try to lead people away from belief in Jesus Christ and into the corrupt worship of the first beast. Those who refuse to give the first beast their praise will be singled out for punishment. He will have the same authority given to him by Satan as the first beast was given.

The healing of his *death-stroke* is so that it looks like the Messiah!

"And he doeth great signs, that he should even make fire to come down out of heaven upon the earth in the sight of man" (verse thirteen).

The goal of the dragon, the first beast, and the second beast is to promote idolatrous worship of themselves. One of their strategies will be to deceive people into following the first beast by performing "miraculous signs." This will put the second beast on par with the prophets of God. This second beast will have counterfeit attributes of a prophet, and many have labeled him as the "false prophet."

The ability of Satan-inspired prophets to perform deceiving miracles is attested to elsewhere in Scripture. For instance: Deuteronomy 13:1–5; Matthew 7:22; 24: 24; Mark 13:22; 2 Thessalonians 2:9, and Revelation 16:14 and 19:20.

The ability to distinguish between true and false prophets has always been difficult but not impossible. The followers of Jesus Christ have been given the gift of discernment, and we must constantly be alert to discern the spirits (1 John 4:1–3).

The fire from heaven could refer to the incident in 1 Kings 18:38, where the prophet Elijah called down fire from heaven. A second reference could be to the fire that came down on the heads of the apostles on the day of Pentecost (Acts 2:3). Either way, this is a definite attempt to counterfeit acts of God in the past.

> And he deceiveth them that dwell on the earth by reason of the signs which it was given him to do in the sight of the beast; saying to them that dwell on the earth, that they should make an image to the beast who hath the stroke of the sword and lived.
>
> Verse fourteen

"Deceive" is the Bible's term for the activity of false teachers who lead people to worship gods other than the true and living God. Now the second beast orders the setting up of an image, or statue, of the first beast! The image is not a mere copy but indicates that it is real.

> And it was given unto him to give breath to it, even to the image to the beast, and that the image of the beast should both speak, and cause that as many as should not worship the image of the beast should be killed.
>
> Verse fifteen

The King James Bible translation reads, "And he had power to give life unto the image of the beast." The English word "life" in these translations is in error. The translation should be "breath," Greek *pneuma*. What should be clear is that the second beast did not give life to the statue but gave the appearance that it was alive. God is the only One who can give life! Like the pagan magicians of the Old Testament, the second beast will be able to perform sleight of hand, which will deceive many.

The early church father, Irenaeus, spoke on this point, "Let no one imagine that he performs these wonders by divine power, but by the working of magic." We should not be surprised if, since the demons and unholy spirits are at his service, he, through their means, do tricks that will lead the inhabitants of the world astray.

I'll refer to David Copperfield as the present-day magician that we see on television, who made the Boeing 747 airliner disappear on stage. He didn't actually make it disappear but used an elaborate scheme to make it appear as though it did. This will be similar.

With its ability to move, speak, and give the appearance of being alive, this statue will be considered a god. The statue will be set up in a public place, and everyone will be required to worship it. The statue will be "wired for sound" and will address people who approach it.

There will be a requirement for everyone to worship the statue, and anyone who refuses will be killed.

"And he causeth all, the small and the great, and the rich and the poor, and the free and the bond, that there be given them a mark on their right hand, or on their forehead" (verse sixteen).

He will reorganize the world's population. We see six classes of people here: the small, the great, the rich, the poor, the free, and the slaves. All of the people on the earth will be forced to receive a mark or brand on their right hand or on their forehead.

A brand signifies ownership and, in biblical times, was used as a means of identification of slaves as well as animals. Therefore, this mark will identify the wearer of the mark as belonging to the devil.

The number 666 represents one six for each of the three: the devil, the first beast, and the second beast. If we use God's number for God the Father, God the Son, and God the Holy Spirit, we have 777, or one seven for each of the three. That is, 777 is the triune God, which we call the Trinity. So, 666 is the devil's attempt to bring on his counterfeit trinity.

So finally, we have the devil, who wants to be God, the first beast who wants to be Christ, and the second beast who wants to be the Holy Spirit, the unholy trinity!

Anyone, therefore, who takes this mark thereby bears testimony to his allegiance to the infernal trinity.

For many years, Christians have worried about whether or not they could resist this "mark of the beast." But for a Christian, there is no need to worry. We will not be here! We will be with Jesus in heaven for the entire time.

Chapter Fourteen

"And I saw, and behold, the Lamb standing on the mount Zion, and with him a hundred and forty and four thousand, having his name, and the name of his Father, written on their foreheads" (verse one).

John now sees another scene before him. There is a Lamb standing on Mount Zion. It is *the* Lamb, or Jesus! Standing with him are 144,000 who have His name and the name of God the Father written on their foreheads. These are the 144,000 we saw in chapter seven, verses four and five. We saw in chapter nine, verse four, that they were sealed on their foreheads! And now, we see what the seal was: the names of Jesus and Yahweh, or God the Father.

A question arises: Why do they have Jesus' name on their foreheads? When they were selected from the twelve tribes, Jesus and His church had left the earth. Had they, at this time, accepted Jesus as their Messiah? From the text, we cannot know the answer to this question.

"And I heard a voice from heaven, as the voice of many waters, and as the voice of a great thunder: and the voice which I heard was the voice of harpers harping with their harps" (verse two).

Next, John hears a sound (Greek phonan, where we get our word "phonograph," or "sound writer") coming from heaven. This was a loud, musical sound, and the sound was like many harps being played and the harpists singing as they played.

> And they sing as it were a new song before the throne, and before the four living creatures and the elders: and no man could learn the song save the hundred and forty and four thousand, even they that had been purchased out of the earth.
>
> Verse three

They were singing a song that had never been heard before. Standing before the throne of God, the four living creatures, the elders, and the harpists taught the song to the 144,000 who had been sealed and saved.

We now get a little more information about the 144,000. They have learned a new song that they alone would ever learn. From the context, this is the only place the song would ever be sung.

> These are they that were not defiled with women; for they are virgins. These are they that follow the Lamb whithersoever he goeth. These were purchased from among men, to be the firstfruits unto God and unto the Lamb.
>
> Verse four

Again, we are given more information about the 144,000. They are males, virgins, and they follow Jesus wherever He goes. They are the firstfruits, or the first of many people to be saved during the Tribulation period.

"And in their mouth was found no lie: they were without blemish" (verse five).

These men speak only the truth. "No lie" refers to the blasphemy of the beast worshippers who deny the Father and the Son and believe the beast and worship his image. In other words, they have no faults at all.

So, to date: the 144,000 are all Jews. They are all males. They are sealed on their foreheads. The seal is in the names of Jesus and Yahweh. There are 12,000 of them from each of the twelve tribes of Israel. They are all virgins. They never live. They have no faults at all. The group as a whole has remained faithful to God. They are the first men saved during the Tribulation period. They follow Jesus wherever He goes. They sing a new song that no one else will ever learn.

And if I remember correctly, this is all of the information there is in Scripture concerning them. Please notice there are those who say these 144,000 are witnesses for Jesus. We even have a religion that calls itself the 144,000 witnesses for Jehovah. These are called Jehovah's Witnesses. However, nowhere in the Bible are these sealed men called witnesses!

And a little bit more trivia for you: "Jehovah" is not a good translation for God's name. His name is Yahweh. When the Germans translated the Scriptures from Hebrew to German, their Y became a J, and their W became a V. In the Hebrew language, there are no vowels, only consonants. The Jews added markings to letters to help with pronunciation. These marks are called "vowel points." The vowel point representing the letter *A* was mistakenly changed to an *E*, and the vowel point representing the *E* became an *A*. Therefore, the name "Yahweh" became "Jehovah" in the German language and was transliterated into English using the same letters.

I mentioned this just to show you how a little error can grow into a big error. I ask you: How many people are there who worship in this perverted religion without even realizing they're wrong? The next time you meet one of the Jehovah's Witnesses, show them how they have been duped! Ask them what Jewish tribe they are from, and even better than that, who marked them. And how come they were chosen since this will not happen until the Tribulation period?

"And I saw another angel flying in mid heaven, having eternal good tidings to proclaim unto them that dwell on the earth, and unto every nation and tribe and tongue and people" (verse six).

This section now moves from the scene of triumph to the final judgments on the enemies of the Lamb. This angel is flying in the earth's atmosphere, where he will proclaim the gospel message to everyone who lives on the earth. No one will be left out. Every living soul will hear this message. This is the *good tidings!*

"And he saith with a great voice, Fear God, and give him glory; for the hour of his judgment is come: and worship him that made the heaven and the earth and sea and fountains of waters" (verse seven).

This angel then gives his warning message. His reference is to the final time of judgment that is about to fall on them.

They have this last chance to give God the glory He deserves and worship Him. He is the true God. He is the Creator. He alone is worthy to receive their worship.

"And another, a second angel, followed, saying, Fallen, fallen is Babylon the great, that hath made all the nations to drink of the wine of the wrath of her fornication" (verse eight).

A second angel, in anticipation of what is to come, announces the demise of Babylon. Babylon is the anti-God system of idolatry. It is this idolatry that causes men to deny God. It is the same system of idolatry that has been in existence since Lucifer decided that he wanted to be god and caused the fall of man. It is this idolatry that Nimrod brought into the world in human form.

This Babylon (some translations say that this is a city, but the Greek does not!) is the woman who was transported in a basket in the prophecy of Zechariah 5:5–11 and who is referred to as the whore of Babylon.

This system of false religion will incur the results of her perversion of the Word of God and His worship.

"And another angel, a third, followed them, saying with a great voice, If any man worshippeth the beast and his image, and receiveth a mark on his forehead, or upon his hand" (verse nine).

Here we see a third angel flying through the sky to deliver another message to the people on the earth. You know, if I had seen the first and second angels, I think I would have been awakened, and here comes the third.

And this message would be enough to frighten even the strongest of men. Just suppose that I was one of those who worshipped the beast and had taken his mark. What would I do?

> He also shall drink of the wine of the wrath of God, which is prepared unmixed in the cup of his anger; and he shall be tormented with fire and brimstone in the presence of the holy angels, and in the presence of the Lamb.
>
> Verse ten

I would have to take the entire wrath of God. This unmixed wrath hasn't a drop of mercy in it. It is God's pure anger and will be delivered with the fire and brimstone of hell.

While this is happening, the holy angels of Jesus Christ will be watching. To know that you had a choice and didn't have to face the punishment will only make it more terrible.

"And the smoke of their torment goeth up forever and ever; and they have no rest day and night, they that worship the beast and his image, and whoso receiveth the mark of his name" (verse eleven).

Now we come to the point of this book that gives us a picture of the extent of the punishment of the unsaved. As they are tormented with fire and brimstone, they will burn continually in this fire, day and night, for all of eternity! There is never a letup in their punishment. Their flesh will go up in smoke; their bones will burn, and then it will be regenerated and start over again. They have taken the mark of the beast, have worshipped him, and for that, they will burn in the lake of fire forever.

There are those who believe that there will be an end to God's wrath eventually, but this verse definitely shows this not to be the case.

"Here is the patience of the saints, they that keep the commandments of God, and the faith of Jesus" (verse twelve).

Despite the threat of the beast and the false prophet, there will be those who, if they listen to this warning and keep the commandments of God, will avoid this punishment. This is the same as the message in Matthew 24:13 (KJV), which says, "He that shall endure unto the end, the same shall be saved." The Greek word for "patience" should be translated "into," that is, *hupomonan*.

Even though refusing the mark of the beast will cause death, death is preferred over eternal damnation.

> And I heard the voice from heaven saying, Write, Blessed are the dead who die in the Lord from henceforth: yea, saith the Spirit, that they may rest from their labors; for their works follow with them.
>
> Verse thirteen

Notice something here that is very important: there is a voice emanating from heaven. It is the voice of the Holy Spirit. This implies that the Holy Spirit is no longer the Comforter on the earth. When the church is transported away from the earth to heaven, the Holy Spirit departs also.

The Holy Spirit is the Restrainer of the man of lawlessness (2 Thessalonians 3:1–8), and it is only after the church and the Holy Spirit are removed from the earth that the devil will have free rein.

Those who decide to turn their lives over to God and refuse the mark of the beast will be killed, but their deaths are their entrance into heaven and eternal life with God. They will be judged for what they do during the Tribulation period before they are killed, and their labors will be credited to them.

We see this same thing in Matthew 25:31–46.

> But when the Son of man shall come in his glory, and all the angels with him, then shall he sit on the throne of his glory: and before him shall be gathered all the nations: and he shall separate them one from another, as the shepherd separateth the sheep from the goats; and he shall set the sheep on his right hand, but the goats on the left. Then shall the King say unto them on his right hand, Come, ye blessed of my Father, inherit the kingdom prepared for you from the foundation of the world: for I was hungry, and ye gave me to eat; I was thirsty, and ye gave me drink; I was a stranger, and ye took me in; naked, and ye clothed me; I was sick, and ye visited me; I was in prison, and ye came unto me. Then shall the righteous answer him, saying, Lord, when saw we thee hungry, and fed thee? or athirst, and gave thee drink? And when saw we thee a stranger, and took thee in? or naked, and clothed thee? And when saw we thee sick, or in prison, and came unto thee? And the King shall answer and say unto them, Verily I say to you, Inasmuch as ye did it unto one of these my brethren, even these least, ye did it unto me. Then shall he say

also unto them on the left hand, Depart from me, ye cursed, into the eternal fire which is prepared for the devil and his angels: for I was hungry, and ye did not give me to eat; I was thirsty, and ye gave me no drink; I was a stranger, and you took me not in; naked, and ye clothed me not; sick, and in prison, and ye visited me not. Then shall they also answer, saying, Lord, when saw we thee hungry, or athirst, or a stranger, or naked, or sick, or in prison, and did not minister unto thee? Then shall he answer them, saying, Verily I say unto you, Inasmuch as ye did it not unto one of these least, ye did it not unto me. And these shall go away into eternal punishment: but the righteous into eternal life.

I am positive that most of you have heard this verse used incorrectly to say that we should care for the needy of the world. And I agree with this premise, but I disagree with using this verse of Scripture to prove the point.

God's people are the righteous Jews! How they are cared for and treated during the Tribulation period is the requirement for entry into the millennial kingdom of Jesus Christ. If His people are treated kindly and sustained in the face of death by the devil and his cronies, those who help them, the sheep, will enter into the kingdom.

"And I saw, and behold, a white cloud; and on the cloud I saw one sitting like unto a son of man, having on his head a golden crown, and in his hand sharp sickle" (verse fourteen).

Now John observes a white cloud. There was someone sitting on this cloud, someone who had the appearance of a man.

This man wore a golden crown. This is a victor's crown (Greek: stephanon). The crown is not a ruler's crown (Greek: diadema). This description is the same as in Revelation 1:13 and is there identified as being Jesus. There is a problem in identifying this one who has the appearance of a man because, in the next verse, we see an angel giving what appears to be a command.

The sharp sickle is the tool of a farmer. It is used to harvest grain. Here, the context is the harvest of the unrighteous.

> And another angel came out from the temple, crying with a great voice to him that sat on the cloud, Send forth thy sickle, and reap: for the hour to reap is come; for the harvest of the earth is ripe.
>
> Verse fifteen

Still, another angel comes from the Temple and cries loudly for the one sitting on the cloud to send his sickle to the earth because the time has come for the harvest. This shows that God's wrath comes from His holiness and from His throne room. Everything that has to be accomplished has been done. There were three other angels mentioned in this chapter in verses six, eight, and nine. This is the fourth who comes out of heaven.

"And he that sat on the cloud cast his sickle on the earth; and the earth was reaped" (verse sixteen).

This is the execution of the command directed by the fourth angel.

"Another angel came out from the temple which is in heaven, he also having a sharp sickle" (verse seventeen).

Yet another angel, the fifth, comes out of the Temple. He, too, was carrying a sharp sickle.

And another angel came out from the altar, he that hath power over fire; and he called with a great voice to him that had the sharp sickle, saying, Send forth thy sharp sickle, and gather the clusters of the vine of the earth; for her grapes are fully ripe.

Verse eighteen

And then a sixth angel comes out from the altar of the Temple. This angel has the power of fire. He calls to the fifth angel, who has a sharp sickle, to send the sickle to the earth to cut off the clusters from the vine of the earth. This is to be understood as the reaping of the evil men who are there. Their sin has become as evil as it can be.

"And the angel cast his sickle into the earth, and gathered the vintage of the earth, and cast it into the winepress, the great winepress, of the wrath of God" (verse nineteen).

When the angel threw his sickle onto the earth, it gathered all of the unsaved together, and he threw them into the winepress, which is the wrath of God. Jeremiah 25:30–33 speaks of this harvest in this way:

Therefore prophesy thou against them all these words, and say unto them, Jehovah will roar from on high, and utter his voice from his holy habitation; he will mightily roar against his fold; he will give a shout, as they that tread the grapes, against all the inhabitants of the earth. A noise shall come even to the end of the earth; for Jehovah hath a controversy with the nation; he will enter into judgment with all flesh: as for the wicked, he will give them to the sword, saith Jehovah. Thus saith Jehovah of hosts, Behold, evil shall go forth from nation to nation, and a great tempest shall be raised up from the uttermost parts of the earth. And the slain of Jehovah shall be at that day from one end of the earth even unto the other end of the earth: they shall not be lamented, neither gathered, nor buried; they shall be dung upon the face of the ground.

Isaiah 63:1–6 says the same thing:

Who is this that cometh from Edom, with dyed garments from Bozrah? this that is glorious in his apparel, marching in the greatness of his strength? I that speak in righteousness, mighty to save. Wherefore art thou red in thine apparel, and thy garments like him that treadeth in the winevat? I have trodden the winepress alone; and of the peoples there was no man with me: yea, I trod them in mine anger, and trampled them in my wrath; And their lifeblood is sprinkled upon my garments, and I have stained all my raiment. For the day of vengeance was in my heart, and the year of my redeemed is come. And I looked, and there was none to help; and I wondered that there was none to uphold: therefore, mine own arm brought salvation unto me; and my wrath, it upheld me. And I trod down the peoples in mine anger, and made them drunk in my wrath, and I poured out their lifeblood in the earth.

Later, in Revelation 19:11–15, we see a description of Jesus:

> And I saw the heaven opened; and behold, a white horse, and he that sat thereon called Faithful and True; and in righteousness he doth judge and make war. And his eyes are a flame of fire, and upon his head are many diadems; and he hath a name written which no one knoweth but he himself. And he is arrayed in a garment sprinkled with blood: and his name is called the Word of God. And the armies which are in heaven followed him upon white horses, clothed in fine linen, white and pure. And out of his mouth proceedeth a sharp sword, that with it he should smite the nations: and he shall rule them with a rod of iron: and he treadeth the winepress of the fierceness of the wrath of God, the Almighty.

This tells us exactly who will be treading the winepress of God's wrath; it will be Jesus!

Joel 3:9–16 has almost the same thing to say about the winepress:

> Proclaim ye this among the nations; prepare war; stir up the mighty men; let all the men of war draw near, let them come up. Beat your plowshares into swords, and your pruning-hooks into spears: let the weak say,

I am strong. Hast ye, and come, all ye nations round about, and gather yourselves together: thither cause thy mighty ones to come down, O Jehovah. Let the nations bestir themselves, and come up to the valley of Jehoshaphat; for there will I sit to judge all of the nations round about. Put ye in the sickle; for the harvest is ripe: come, tread ye; for the winepress is full, the vats overflow; for their wickedness is great. Multitudes in the valley of decision! For the day of Jehovah's near in the valley of decision. The sun and the moon are darkened, and the stars withdraw their shining. And Jehovah will roar from Zion, and utter his voice from Jerusalem; and the heavens and the earth shall shake.

This reaping is referred to as the battle of Armageddon elsewhere.

"And the winepress was trodden without the city, and there came out blood from the winepress, even unto the bridles of the horses, as far as a thousand and six furlongs" (verse twenty).

Putting the Old Testament and New Testament prophecies together will begin in the city of Bozrah, the chief city of Edom. The result of this terrible wrath will be blood flowing from the city for a distance of some 200 miles.

The blood will flow for this 200 miles and will be approximately four to five feet deep, as high as the bridle of a horse. This is about chest type for me.

Note: Israel isn't that big, so it must change in size. Zechariah 14:4–7 says,

And his feet shall stand in that day upon the mount of Olives, which is before Jerusalem on the east; and the mount of Olives shall be cleft in the midst thereof toward the east and toward the west, and there shall be a very great valley; and half of the mountain shall remove towards the north, and half of it toward the south. And ye shall flee by the valley of my mountains; for the valley of the mountains shall reach unto Azel; yea, ye shall flee, like as ye fled from before the earthquake in the days of Uzziah king of Judah; and Jehovah my God shall come, and all the holy ones with thee. And it shall come to pass in that day, that there shall not be light; the bright ones shall withdraw themselves: but it shall be one day which is known unto Jehovah; not day, and not night; but it shall come to pass, that at evening time there shall be light.

When Jesus returns to the earth, he will stand on the Mount of Olives, and it will split open. The entire topography will change dramatically. Little Israel will become huge Israel. Isaiah prophesies that when Jesus returns, there will be great earthquakes. In fulfilling this prophecy, God will change everything.

One final note on chapter fourteen: in this chapter, the events described will cover the entire three and a half years of the Tribulation period. It will cover the events from the sixth trumpet until the coming of the Lord in judgment.

Chapter Fifteen

"And I saw another sign in heaven, great and marvelous, seven angels having seven plagues, which are the last, for in them is finished the wrath of God" (verse one).

In this chapter, we have another sign in heaven. This sign is huge and awesome. I would like to draw your attention to the two words used here: "great" and "marvelous." We have already seen the seven seal judgments, and we are now in the seventh-trumpet judgment; just how much worse could it possibly get? Yet, the language is such that it appears the worst is still to come. What we have seen so far is only child's play compared to what is next!

Here we see seven angels holding seven plagues. Thinking back to the Old Testament: Egypt was wiped out by the plagues brought upon them when the pharaoh wouldn't let the Israelites leave captivity. They still haven't recovered thousands of years later. But here, these angels carry plagues that will be the culmination of the anger poured out by the almighty God.

The importance of the word "anger" is not to be misunderstood. Your translation may read "wrath," but in Greek, the word is thumos and not orge. "Wrath," or orge, is the inner emotion, but anger is an outburst of inner feeling. Thumos is where we get our English word, "thermos," or heat. We will now see the heat of God's anger in its fullness.

These plagues are the most devastating and intense of all those we have seen.

> And I saw as it were a sea of glass mingled with fire; and them that come off victorious from the beast, and from his image, and from the number of his name, standing by the sea of glass, having harps of God.
>
> Verse two

Back in Revelation 4:6, we saw this sea of glass, but now we see it mingled with fire. This tells of the persecution that the saints were subjected to by Satan and his minions. The fire is symbolic of purification. These pure ones have come to the sea of glass and have won the victory against Satan. They were strong enough to refuse to take the mark of the beast, and they refused to worship his statue, and now they stand before the throne of God, holding golden harps.

> And they sing the song of Moses the servant of God, and the song of the Lamb, saying, Great and marvelous are thy works, O Lord God, the Almighty; righteous and true are thy ways, thou King of the ages.
>
> Verse three

These harpists now sing the song of Moses. If you want to learn this song, it is in Deuteronomy 32:1–43. This song tells of

God's deliverance, salvation, and faithfulness. Moses wrote it and taught it to the congregation. As to the song of the Lamb, it is the praise to Jesus which we saw in Revelation 5:9–12.

"Who shall not fear, O Lord, and glorify thy name? For thou art holy; for all the nations shall come and worship before thee; for thy righteous acts have been made manifest" (verse four).

Today there is little reverential fear of God, even among believers. Reverence and glory are due only to our holy God. Therefore, every man, woman, and child will stand before God and get down on their knees before Him.

One reason that the nations will worship God is because He is holy. The word used here is not the usual word used in Scripture for "holy." The Greek word used here is *hosios*, which means that God is absolutely right in vindicating persecuted believers and judging the wicked.

The day has come when all people acknowledge that God's anger, which is about to be poured out, is deserved, righteous, and perfectly designed to achieve His holy purposes. It is notable that the saints in heaven do not sing about their own victory over the beast but about God's sovereignty, glory, and justice.

This knowledge should cause us to take heart, for even if our own nation should continue to move further away from God, the day will come when everyone will know without reserve that God is God!

His acts of wrath are based on righteousness. Now, that righteousness has been demonstrated. He gave us, humans, instructions on how to live our lives and what the penalty was for disobedience. When we see what He has done to those who rejected Him, we should get down on our knees in thanks for saving us from His anger.

"And after these things I saw, and the temple of the tabernacle of the testimony in heaven was opened" (verse five).

John now focuses his attention back on the Temple of God. The heavenly tabernacle opens. That is, the veil of the Holy of Holies opens. This is the place where the Ark of the Covenant, the tablets of the Ten Commandments, and the manna is kept.

"And there came out from the temple the seven angels that had the seven plagues, arrayed with precious stone, pure and bright, and girt about their breasts with golden girdles" (verse six).

The seven angels carrying the seven plagues appear from within the Temple. It is significant to note that even though the plagues emanate from within the Temple, they are to be poured out on men with hearts, hopelessly hardened to sin. Even though God will pardon men at the very last second, His holy attributes and holy character require Him to be just, and therefore, He will punish the obstinate and impertinent.

The angels are wearing bright white linen clothing, and wound about their chests are golden cords, or girdles, which are symbolic of being God's messengers. God is the precious metal of kings. Their girdles are encrusted with precious gemstones.

"And one of the four living creatures gave unto the seven angels seven golden bowls full of the wrath of God, who lived for ever and ever" (verse seven).

John watched as one of the four living creatures handed out the containers that held the anger of God. These bowls are not the deep bowls that are used today. They are shaped more like a saucer, but the emphasis is not on the containers but on the contents!

In the Old Testament, God's wrath, or anger, is pictured as a cup of hot, bitter wine, boiling to the point of overflowing, depicting violent anger from God against sin.

This anger will come from the eternal God, and He will pour out his judgment at the precise and perfect time.

"And the temple was filled with smoke from the glory of God, and from his power; and none was able to enter into the temple, till the seven plagues of the seven angels should be finished" (verse eight).

God's glory has always been seen during the time of His judgment, but in this case, He is concealed in the smoke of His glory until the seven plagues are completed. It will be impossible to enter the Temple until His seething indignation has been completed.

The seven angels now stand ready, awaiting the final signal to pour out the wrath of God!

Chapter Sixteen

"And I heard a great voice out of the temple, saying to the seven angels, Go ye, and pour out the seven bowls of the wrath of God into the earth" (verse one).

As chapter sixteen opens, John hears a great voice emanating from within the Temple. This great voice commands the seven angels to proceed to pour out the bowls of God's wrath upon the earth. Although the voice is not identified, most agree that this is the voice of God. Each angel will pour out his bowl, one by one, in quick succession without further instructions. Without a doubt, what follows is the darkest chapter in the history of mankind.

"And the first went, and poured out his bowl into the earth; and it became a noisome and grievous sore upon the men that had the mark of the beast, and that worshipped his image" (verse two).

When the first angel emptied his bowl, the contents caused disgusting, stinking, foul, filthy boil-like sores to open on everyone who had taken the mark of the beast and had worshipped his statue. These sores were extremely painful and would never heal.

I don't know if you have ever had a blood boil, but when I was a child, they were fairly common. Those things hurt like the dickens. They would not heal until they were opened, and that couldn't be done until they grew to the size where you could see the core of the boil. By that time, you couldn't sleep, and if they were in a bad place, you couldn't even walk. My mom used to get a half-pint bottle and fill it with boiling water. Then she would quickly pour out the water and jam the neck of the hot bottle over the boil. As the heat left the bottle, it caused a vacuum and extracted the core from the boil. After that, the boil would heal.

The sores described here make the blood boils seem like a pimple in comparison.

"And the second poured out his bowl into the sea; and it became blood as of a dead man; And every living soul died, even the things that were in the sea" (verse three).

When the second angel poured out the contents of his bowl, all saltwater seas changed into putrefied blood. That is, the seas will turn into a thick, congealed mass of blood that will stink like a corpse that has lain in the sun for a week or so. This will cause unimaginable disease and death. All of the marine creatures will die. This will severely affect the world's food supply.

"And the third [angel] poured out his bowl into the rivers and the fountains of the waters; and it became blood" (verse four).

When the third angel poured out his bowl of wrath, the freshwater became blood. Every lake, river, stream, spring, well—all the freshwater became putrid. People will dig down in the ground, trying to find water to drink, but will only find more blood.

Without water, people would go mad and stop at nothing to quench their thirst. We can only imagine the agony, panic, and health problems this will bring about. Then comes a great angelic proclamation:

> And I heard the angel of the waters saying, Righteous art thou, who art and wast, thou Holy One, because thou didst thus judge: for they poured out the blood of the saints and the prophets, and blood hast thou given them to drink: they are worthy.
>
> Verses five to six

Often people will question God's judgment upon them, but the angels do not. They confirm that God is justified in pouring out His wrath upon the ungodly. The angel also affirms that the wicked are getting back what they dished out to others. Because of that, they deserve what they are getting.

"And I heard the altar saying, Yea, O Lord God, the Almighty, true and righteous are thy judgments" (verse seven).

Further confirmation is made on this point by a voice emanating from the altar of God. God's judgments are righteous and true.

"And the fourth poured out his bowl upon the sun; and it was given unto it to scorch men with fire" (verse eight).

This judgment is similar to the one in Revelation 8:12, except that there, the sun was darkened. Here the sun will be supernaturally increased by God, causing it to scorch people with fire. There will not be enough shelter to shade people from the intense heat of the sun, and even inside, the sun's rays will pen-

227

etrate and burn the skin. It will be as though everyone will be on a barbecue pit and roasting alive. Huge blisters will form, burst open, and reform. It will be agonizing!

"And men were scorched with great heat: and they blasphemed the name of God who hath the power over these plagues; and they repented not to give him glory" (verse nine).

Instead of the unbelievers crying out to God for mercy, they will curse Him and still not repent of their sins. Not even these terrible events will produce repentance in the hearts of these wicked people.

"And the fifth poured out his bowl upon the throne of the beast; and his kingdom was darkened; and they gnawed their tongues for pain" (verse ten).

Now the fifth angel poured out his bowl of God's wrath. This time God's wrath is poured out on a different target: it is poured out on the throne of the beast. The weather will suddenly go from blistering sunlight to total darkness.

Up to this point, nothing has happened to the false trinity. Now, God will concentrate His wrath on the center of Satan's earthly power. This darkness will be so thick and intense that it will cause severe psychological pain to people already in agony because of their boils and burnt flesh.

The preview of the outer darkness of their eternal abode will cause them to chew on their own tongues for relief from their pain.

"And they blasphemed the God of heaven because of their pains and their sores; and they repented not of their works" (verse eleven).

And they still curse God! They still refuse to repent! Can you imagine this? All it would have taken before all this came down on them was to acknowledge Jesus as their Savior, and they would have been free from this agony. But instead, they gave allegiance to the devil and his cronies and brought all of this on themselves.

"And the sixth poured out his bowl upon the great river, the river Euphrates; and the water thereof was dried up, that the way might be made ready for the kings that come from the sun-rising" (verse twelve).

When the sixth angel poured out his bowl of God's wrath, it was localized. It was poured out on the Euphrates River. The water in the river was dried up completely. This was done so that the river would not be a barrier to the kings who were to come from the east (the sunrising).

The Euphrates is called great because of its location and length. It is the largest and longest river in Western Asia and flows for approximately 1,800 miles, from Syria through Babylon and to the Persian Gulf. The kings from the east will pour across the dried-up river to take part in a battle that we will soon see.

"And I saw coming out of the mouth of the dragon, and out of the mouth of the beast, and out of the mouth of the false prophet, three unclean spirits, as it were frogs" (verse thirteen).

John saw three demonic spirits coming out of the unholy trinity. One from the mouth of Satan, one from the mouth of the antichrist, and one from the mouth of the beast. John says they were like frogs.

"For they are spirits of demons, working signs; which go forth unto the kings of the whole world, to gather them together unto the war of the great day of God, the Almighty" (verse fourteen).

These demonic spirits will perform miracle-like events that will entice the nations east of the Euphrates, and indeed of the whole world, to come and join in the war against God.

"Behold, I come as a thief. Blessed is he that watcheth, and keepeth his garments, lest he walked naked, and they see his shame" (verse fifteen).

This will set the stage for climactic conflict with Jesus at His second coming. Jesus will come very quickly. Matthew 24:27 says, "For as the lightning cometh forth from the east, and is seen even unto the west; so shall be the coming of the Son of man." When Jesus returns, there will be no warning of His coming. When the timing is perfect, He will suddenly appear. He tells everyone that He is coming like a thief. All had better be watching for Him and be ready for His appearing.

"And they gathered them together into the place which is called in Hebrew Har-magedon" (verse sixteen).

The kings of the east will pour across the dried-up Euphrates River and rally at the valley of Armageddon. Mount Megiddo will be their focal point. This mountain is at the uppermost point of the valley of Megiddo.

"And the seventh poured out his bowl upon the air; and there came forth a great voice out of the temple, from the throne, saying, It is done" (verse seventeen).

When the seventh bowl of God's wrath was poured out, John heard this same great voice coming from God's Temple and from His throne with the proclamation, "It is done!" What is done? All of God's wrath has now been poured out upon the earth and its inhabitants!

"And there were lightnings, and voices, and thunders; and there was a great earthquake, such as was not since there were men upon the earth, so great an earthquake, so mighty" (verse eighteen).

Immediately John heard lightning, thunder, and voices come from heaven, and there was an earthquake like none had ever seen or heard of. The earth will convulse in an unprecedented magnitude, causing great damage, disruption, death, and distress on mankind.

> And the great city was divided into three parts, and the cities of the nations fell: and Babylon the great was remembered in the sight of God, to give unto her the cup of the wine of the fierceness of his wrath.
>
> Verse nineteen

Cities worldwide will be destroyed. Jerusalem will be divided into three parts. Babylon was brought to God's sight, and she was to receive her cup of His wrath.

"And every island fled away, and the mountains were not found" (verse twenty).

If you look at a map of Israel and put Jerusalem at its center, then, going in every direction from Jerusalem, you will find that in order to get to some countries, you will have to cross water. In ancient times, any land that had to be approached across the water was referred to as an island. Every continent not joined to Asia will disappear during these awful earthquakes. Every mountain will be leveled. The earth's topography will be radically altered, causing widespread destruction. Billions will be killed.

And great hail, every stone about the weight of a talent, cometh down out of heaven upon men: and men blasphemed God because of the plague of the hail; for the plague thereof is exceeding great.

Verse twenty-one

The climate will change. Weather events never imagined will become commonplace. Even hail falling will be catastrophic. Hailstones weighing a hundred pounds will fall. And guess what? Men will continue to blaspheme and curse God! Even when Satan's world empires are crushed, men will still not repent.

Chapter Seventeen

And there came one of the seven angels that had the seven bowls, and spake with me saying, Come hither, I will show thee the judgment of the great harlot that sitteth upon many waters; with whom the kings of the earth committed fornication, and they that dwell in the earth were made drunken with the wine of her fornication.

Verses one to two

One of the seven angels who had poured out the seven bowls of God's wrath came and spoke to John. He asked John to follow him where he would show him the judgment of the "great harlot who sits upon many waters." The word "harlot" comes from the Greek word *porneia*, which is defined as pornographic in nature: fornication, adultery, prostitution, etc.

This *harlot* is sitting upon many waters! That is, she is sitting upon "peoples, and multitudes, and nations, and tongues" (verse fifteen).

This harlot had captivated the attention and had allied herself with rulers of the entire earth. They became intoxicated with her charm, power, and corrupt ways.

We will see the identity of this harlot in the verses to follow.

"And he carried me away in the Spirit into a wilderness: and I saw a woman sitting upon a scarlet-colored beast, full of names of blasphemy, having seven heads and ten horns" (verse three).

The angel transports John in the spirit into a wilderness area where he sees a strange sight. He sees a woman sitting on a bright red beast. This beast has seven heads, ten horns and is covered with blasphemous names.

> And the woman was arrayed in purple and scarlet, and decked with gold and precious stone and pearls, having in her hand a golden cup full of abominations, even the unclean things of her fornication.
>
> Verse four

This system (called the harlot) presents a look of ostentatious extravagance. She is decked out in robes of purple and red, decorated with gold and precious gemstones. Yet, along with her beautiful and wealthy appearance, this *harlot* is carrying a cup filled with abominations and the filthiness of her fornications.

In the Bible, the word "fornication" is used to express idolatrous worship and the immoral practices associated with it. Here it expresses the *harlot's* poisonous cup of idolatry that will lead to the destruction of her and those who follow her. This is a system of religion that would become prominent during the Tribulation period. We do not know a lot about how this religion will surface and become so prominent. We only know that it will come out in the open after the Christians have been taken to heaven in the rapture of the church. One thing is for sure: it is the pagan and idolatrous religion that has been in existence since it was established by Nimrod.

"And upon her forehead a name written, MYSTERY, BABYLON THE GREAT, THE MOTHER OF THE HARLOTS AND OF THE ABOMINATIONS OF THE EARTH" (verse five).

The name on her forehead is like the headbands worn by Roman prostitutes in the first century BC to advertise their profession. This *harlot*, though, is advertising to us that she is a religious system that has allied with the devil. This religion is the one that formulated pagan idolatry and worship. The word "mystery" refers to something that has always been hidden but is now being revealed for all to see.

The religion is that which originated in Babylon and has continued in one form or another down to us today, and at the time of the Tribulation period will be the only religious system allowed.

This diabolical religious system can be traced back to the city in which Nimrod built the tower of Babel, later called Babylon. This tower was known to be a center and symbol of man's pride and rebellion against God.

This religious system branched out into other nations where similar towers, or ziggurats, were built to honor the variant heathen deities. History records that Semiramis, Nimrod's wife, became the head priestess of this religious system known as Babylonian Mysteries.

This religion eventually found a home in Asia Minor and thrived there. We read of this religion when we examined the seven churches of Asia Minor in chapters three and four. This religion was eventually headquartered in Rome.

The chief priests wore a head covering called a miter that was shaped like the head of a fish with its mouth open. Jewels were attached to each side of the miter to resemble eyes. This headdress was worn in honor of Dagon, the fish god, the pagan lord of life.

In Rome, the chief priest took the title pontifex maximus, which means "bridge maker." Originally this meant that the chief priest was the bridge between Christianity and paganism. This person was responsible for mixing Christian and pagan beliefs so as to make them palatable for everyone. We use another word today to show the same thing, "ecumenical." This is a present-day movement to achieve worldwide unity among religions through greater cooperation and improved understanding. Yet another word for this is "compromise"!

Over time, the church in Rome adopted many of the Babylonian practices and idolatrous teaching and, in doing so, obscured the true meaning of the Scriptures. Among those were the teaching of baptismal regeneration, the saying of the Mass, the rituals of processions, and the worship of the Virgin Mary.

Many of their teachings can be attributed to Constantine, who was so taken with Christianity that he decreed that everyone would become a Christian. He then adopted Christianity as the state religion, and what man would say he was not a Christian if it was the law of the land, and you could be killed for not becoming a Christian?

Today, a large number of Protestant denominations have either turned a blind eye and a deaf ear to the antibiblical teachings of the Roman Catholic Church or are cooperating with them in various religious functions.

This will eventually, and ultimately, give birth to a one-world church after the rapture of the true believers.

"And I saw the woman drunken with the blood of the saints, and with the blood of the martyrs of Jesus. And when I saw her, I wondered with a great wonder" (verse six).

During the Tribulation period, the heretical church will not tolerate competition from other beliefs, nor will she stand still for those who will not agree with her beliefs. Therefore, she will pour out cruelties against the defenseless Tribulation saints. She will cause them to be beheaded, and she will be inflamed with lust for more violence and inhumane savagery as she attempts to destroy all knowledge of Christ and His followers.

The antichrist will assist her by providing the political power to carry out this persecution.

John was stunned by what he had seen. He stood there in astonishment.

"And the angel said unto me, wherefore didst thou wonder? I will tell thee the mystery of the woman, and of the beast that carrieth her, which hath the seven heads and the ten horns" (verse seven).

The angel responded to John's disbelief. He asked, "Why do you wonder about what is happening? I will tell you about this harlot. I will reveal her mystery! I will also tell you about the beast that supports her, that is, the beast with the seven heads and the ten horns."

> The beast that thou sawest was, and is not; and is about to come up out of the abyss, and to go into perdition. And they that dwell on the earth shall wonder,

they whose name hath not been written in the book
of life from the foundation of the world, when they
behold the beast, how that he was, and is not, and
shall come.

Verse eight

We see here a thumbnail picture of the three-stage history of the beast. The play on tenses, "was," "is not," and "shall come," refers to Satan, who once had unchallenged power over the earth. He was defeated by Jesus at Calvary, and before his final sentence to destruction, will again be given power over the earth, but this time it will not go unchallenged. He will be defeated and will go into the everlasting fire.

In the revival of Satan's power and authority during the Tribulation period, he will deceive the unsaved inhabitants of the earth, and they will readily and gladly follow him in awe. These are the inhabitants of the earth who did not have their names written in the Lamb's book of life.

"Here is the mind that hath wisdom. The seven heads are the seven mountains, on which the woman sitteth" (verse nine).

This verse is a challenge to those who think! Wisdom is the proper use of knowledge. The angel gave John the knowledge to pass on to us, and we must use that knowledge properly. The angel now proceeds to explain the vision that John has seen. He tells John that the seven heads of the beast are seven mountains.

Now I must take some time to explain these seven mountains: there are those who have misinterpreted the Greek word *ora* as "hill." *Ora* is properly translated into English as "mountain." The Greek word for "hill" is *bounos*. In misinterpreting ora as "hill," these people have spiritualized this chapter of the book of Revelation! They have come to the conclusion that the "seven mountains" are *seven hills* and that the *seven hills* are the *seven hills* of Rome, and thereby represent the Roman Empire that has been revived and will be the seventh world empire.

They go on to try to prove their theory by forcing Roman emperors into their mold, using five of them who died violent deaths. I could go on, but all we have to do is look at the next verse, and we will see what the seven mountains represent.

"And they are seven kings; the five are fallen, the one is, the other is not yet come; and when he cometh, he must continue a little while" (verse ten).

Under Satan's rule and under pagan religion, seven Gentile kings will rule over Israel. In AD 95, when this book was written, five of these rulers had already fallen, or died: the kings of Egypt, Assyria, Babylon, Medo-Persia, and Greece. The one who is, or the one who was in power over Israel in AD 95, was the emperor of Rome. The seventh is yet to come!

These seven empires cover the history of the Gentile world rule and their domination of Israel until their destruction by Jesus Christ at His second coming.

"And the beast that was, and is not, is himself also an eighth, and is of the seven; and he goes into perdition" (verse eleven).

Further revelation is given to John. The beast, which we just described, is to be the eighth ruler of the world. But he comes out of the seventh empire.

His destiny is perdition. This eighth king will be destroyed by Jesus Christ at His second coming and will be cast into the abyss.

"And the ten horns that thou sawest are ten kings, who have received no kingdom as yet; But they receive authority as kings, with the beast, for one hour" (verse twelve).

The seventh empire will be ruled by a *ten-kingdom confederacy*. In the present, there are no such kingdoms. During the Tribulation period, they will come into existence and be given the power to rule the world. They will receive their power and authority as kings from the beast. And look at the Scripture text and see how long they will be in power: one hour, sixty short minutes, and then the antichrist will take over! He will manifest complete dictatorial power, which will introduce the eighth, or final Gentile world rule.

"These have one mind, and they give their power and authority unto the beast" (verse thirteen).

Actually, these seven kings will have no say in the matter. They will be titular at best. That is, they will be kings in the name only, and they will respond to the antichrist by surrendering their offices with no resistance.

"These shall war against the Lamb, and the Lamb shall overcome them, for he is Lord of lords, and King of kings; and they also shall overcome that are with him, called the chosen and faithful" (verse fourteen).

Because these kingdoms will not rule independently but will be confederate (with one mind), they will do the bidding of the antichrist. Collectively they will go along with him, even to the final battle with Jesus, who will be the ultimate victor. Along with Jesus will come an army of the faithful who will share in Jesus' victorious conquest.

"And he saith unto me, The waters which thou sawest, where the harlot sitteth, are peoples, and multitudes, and nations, and tongues" (verse fifteen).

The harlot's system will have influence worldwide by the middle of the Tribulation period. Those whom she will impact are described as waters, symbolic of all people in the world. By this time, all the world's population will have become submissive to her seductive lure, being made drunk with the wine of her heathen religious teaching and worship.

"And the ten horns which thou sawest, and the beast, these shall hate the harlot, and shall make her desolate and naked, come and shall eat her flesh, and shall burn her utterly with fire" (verse sixteen).

An abrupt turnaround will take place as the ten horns become aware of the influence the harlot exerts. Their earlier love for the religion of the harlot will turn to bitter hate. Her charm and seduction will have lost their magnetism. They will turn on her suddenly, take away all of her wealth, and strip her of her support. They will expose her moral corruption, and like wild dogs, they will slaver over her dead corpse. They will totally eliminate every part of her visage so that no one will even remember her.

"For God did put in their hearts to do his mind, and to come to one mind, and to give their kingdom unto the beast, until the words of God should be accomplished" (verse seventeen).

God will initiate this hostile action against the pseudoreligious system. The kings will think they are carrying out their own program for conquest, but they will actually accomplish God's plan.

If you would like to see where these ten kingdoms are located, turn your Bible to Psalm 83:1–8 (KJV):

> Keep not thou silence, O God: hold not thy peace, and be not still, O God. For, lo, thine enemies make a tumult: and they that hate thee have lifted up the head. They have taken crafty counsel against thy people, and consulted against the hidden ones. They have said, Come, and let us cut them off from being a nation; that the name of Israel may be no more in remembrance. For they have consulted together with one consent: they are confederate against thee: The tabernacles of Edam, and the Ishmaelites; of Moab, and the Hagarenes; Gebal, and Ammon, and Amalek; The Philistines with the inhabitants of Tyre; Assur also is joined with them: they have holpen the children of Lot. Selah.

In psalm eighty-three, ten groups of people have formed an alliance against Israel. They have come together to war against the Jews. They have decided that they have to get rid of the Jews once and for all.

These are ten nations who hate Israel so deeply that they will put aside their own differences in order to destroy the Jews.

The time for this is given in verse three, as they plot and plan against God's hidden ones. Back in Revelation 12:6 and 12–14, we saw the first reference to God's hidden ones. They were transported away from the hands of the antichrist and hidden from him for their protection. Now their enemies are plotting against them.

They try to put together a ploy that will trick the Jews into coming out from hiding. If they will, these ten kingdoms will annihilate them. They want to wipe out every man, woman, and child so that the name of Israel and the religion of the Jews will never again be even a part of any of the world's languages.

These ten kingdoms are composed of Arab nations. Ishmael, the only child sired by Abraham, was thought to be the inheritor of the family name and fortune. But when he was thirteen years old, Abraham became the father of a legitimate son, Isaac. Abraham eventually sent his bastard son, Ishmael, and Ishmael's mother, Hagar, from his house. Ishmael was thereby disinherited, and Isaac became Abraham's sole heir. Since that time, there has been hatred between Ishmael's offspring and the offspring of Isaac. This is known to us today as the conflict between the Arabs and the Jews, a conflict that has been going on since the time of Abraham.

If you plot the ten kingdoms listed in psalm eighty-three on a map, you will find that they completely encircle Israel. Every single kingdom spoken of here is composed of the descendants of Ishmael. Incredibly, this is and has been, throughout history, a family feud into which the entire world has been drawn and which will culminate during the Tribulation period. Peace in the Middle East, forget it! There will be none until the second coming of Christ.

"And the woman whom thou sawest is the great city, which reigneth over the kings of the earth" (verse eighteen).

The great city spoken of here is Babylon. There are those who believe that Babylon will be rebuilt in the future. Saddam Hussein began reconstruction of some of the buildings there, but his plans were cut short. Babylon is not necessarily the ancient city rebuilt; however, it could be. This Babylon is a religious system, a one-world religion coming to the fore during the Tribulation period. When this harlot is removed from the scene, the antichrist will set up his own religious system, and the one-world religion will become the worship of Satan.

Considering the direction the world has been taking, there is a movement afoot to introduce a one-world government, as seen in the United Nations, and a move toward one religious system guided by ecumenism.

Like when a new building is erected, the foundation has been laid, and the building blocks are beginning to be put in place!

But in the Tribulation period, the one-world religion will definitely be the ancient religion of Babylon.

Chapter Eighteen

Chapter eighteen opens with John stating, "After these things I saw another angel coming down out of heaven, having great authority; and the earth was lightened with his glory."

The phrase "after these things" indicates that John sees yet another scene opening to him. He sees another angel, the one with a huge amount of authority from God. The countenance of this angel was such that the entire earth was brightened by the glory in which he was enveloped.

> And he cried with a mighty voice, saying, Fallen, fall-
> en is Babylon the great, and is become a habitation
> of demons, and a hold of every unclean spirit, and a
> hold of every unclean and hateful bird.
>
> Verse two

The angel was very loud in his proclamation of the fall of the evil religious system called Babylon. This once-thriving system will be taken over by demons and unclean spirits. All of the unclean and hateful birds will be hovering over false religions like scavengers over carrion.

For by the wine of the wrath of her fornication all the nations are fallen; and the kings of the earth committed fornication with her, and the merchants of the earth waxed rich by the power of her wantonness.

Verse three

One of the reasons for her demise is her decadent relationship with all nations, and she brought it on herself by her wickedness. Because the nations had indulged with her, they, too, have fallen to God's wrath. Those merchants and rulers who joined with her and had become rich off her will also fall with her. Together they will all be subject to God's fury.

The religious system that had satisfied the desires of those who followed the beast and rejected the Lamb of God now faces judgment.

"And I heard another voice from heaven, saying, Come forth, my people, out of her, that ye have no fellowship with her sins, and that you received not of her plagues" (verse four).

This voice is that of God! He commands His true believers to come out of Babylon. They are to disassociate themselves from this evil system of idolatry, luxury, and violence. Those who fail to do so will not be protected when He destroys the system and the city. This same admonishment was given to the Jewish people before the destruction of ancient Babylon (Jeremiah 50:4–8).

Not responding to this command would make a person the partaker of Babylon's sins and the plagues awaiting her.

"For her sins have reached even unto heaven, and God hath remembered her iniquities" (verse five).

God will remember the spiritual and moral evil of Babylon and will judge her accordingly. "Her sins have reached to heaven" is a play on words. This is a comparison to the tower of Babel that began the wicked history of ancient Babylon and was built by Nimrod to reach into heaven (Genesis 11:4).

"Render unto her even as she rendered, and double unto her the double according to her works: in the cup which she mingled, mingle unto her double" (verse six).

The harlot here faces the inevitable law of retribution, or retaliation. In the Mosaic law was the code, an eye for an eye, tooth for tooth, hand for hand, foot for foot, burning for burning, wound for wound, stripe for stripe, or same for same, but here, because of superior knowledge from God and greater guilt, God's judgment will double in severity.

"How much soever she glorified herself, and waxed wanton, so much give her of torment and mourning: for she saith in her heart, I sit a queen, and am no widow, and shall in no wise see mourning" (verse seven).

Here is another instance of the law of retaliation: for self-gratification, there will be sorrow; for luxurious living, there will be torment. The harlot claims to be no widow because her lovers are the kings of the earth. She is like the church in Laodicea, which declared, "I am rich, and increased with goods" and didn't know she was "wretched, and miserable, poor, blind, and naked" (Revelation 3:17, KJV).

Like those in the church who didn't repent, the harlot will be punished more severely than we can even imagine. The leaders of this religious system have put her on a throne, and she feels that she is above reproach. Nothing and no one will ever be able to tell her differently! In her idolatrous faith, only her doctrine is correct. All others are not to be considered.

She says, "I am no widow." This is a reference to Isaiah 47:8. There, the text says that Babylon feels that she will never be exposed to punishment, but she is wrong!

"Therefore in one day shall her plagues come, death, and mourning, and famine; and she shall be utterly burned with fire; for strong as the Lord God who judged her" (verse eight).

When God sends His wrath on the whore of Babylon, it will come fast, hard, and complete! She literally will not know what hit her! Her self-glorification will lead to self-sufficiency, self-deification, and finally, self-deception. Although the kings of the earth glorify her with praise, she will be forsaken by God.

"And the kings of the earth, who committed fornication and lived wantonly with her, shall weep and wail over her, when they look upon the smoke of her burning" (verse nine).

The first group of people who will mourn the death of the religious system will be the kings of the earth who benefited from their allegiance with her. They will beat their chests in woe and cry over her death, for they will no longer benefit from her influence over the earth.

"Standing afar off for the fear of her torment, saying, Woe, woe, the great city, Babylon, the strong city! for in one hour is thy judgment come" (verse ten).

These kings will not lift a hand to help her lest they be drawn into her doom. They will be stunned by the rapidity of the complete destruction of the once great, untouchable, worldwide religion. And it all took place in just sixty minutes!

"And the merchants of the earth weep and mourn over her, for no man buyeth their merchandise anymore" (verse eleven).

The second group to be affected by Babylon's demise are the merchants. This group, which was made rich by their alliance with the heretical church, will suddenly lose their contacts all over the world and be left with no customers. No one would dare buy from them.

> Merchandise of gold, and silver, and precious stone, and pearls, and fine linen, and purple, and silk, and scarlet; and all thyine wood, and every vessel of ivory, and every vessel made of the most precious wood, and of brass, and iron, and marble; and cinnamon, and spice, and incense, and ointment, and frankincense, and wine, and oil, and fine flour, and wheat, and cattle, and sheep; and merchandise of horses and chariots and slaves; and souls of men.
>
> Verses twelve to thirteen

Costly jewelry, clothing, perfumes and ointments, furniture, home decorations, food, pots and pans, spices, gourmet foods, ordinary food, livestock, human servants and slaves, and even the souls of those who have succumbed to the lies of the religious doctrines.

> And the fruits which thy soul lusted after are gone from thee, and all things that were dainty and sumptuous are perished from thee, and men shall find them no more at all. The merchants of these things, who were made rich by her, shall stand afar off for the fear of her torment, weeping and mourning; saying

Woe, woe, the great city, she was that arrayed in fine linen and purple and scarlet, and decked with gold and precious stone and pearl! for in an hour so great riches is made desolate.

Verses fourteen to seventeen

All are going from the grasp of the merchants who plied their goods around the world with no thought to those they were hurting. All of them wept over the death of Babylon, but they wept from afar. Like the kings, their riches evaporated in one hour.

And every shipmaster, and everyone that saileth any wither, and mariners, and as many as gain their living by sea, stood all afar off, and cried out as they looked upon the smoke of her burning, saying, What city is like the great city? And they cast dust on their heads, and cried, weeping and mourning, saying, Woe, woe, the great city, wherein all that had their ships in the sea were made rich by reason of her costliness! for in one hour she is made desolate.

Verses seventeen to nineteen

Third, the mariners will mourn over their loss. Expressing great grief, they echo the outcry of those mentioned earlier. They grieve as those in the Old Testament by putting dust on their heads and crying uncontrollably. They also have lost their worldwide financial head.

"Rejoice over her, thou heaven, and ye saints, and ye apostles, and ye prophets; for God hath judged your judgment on her" (verse twenty).

In contrast to the kings, merchants, and mariners who lament the death of Babylon, heaven, along with holy apostles and prophets, will rejoice over Babylon's destruction. They will rejoice because God has avenged the blood of the saints. He will pay back Babylon with the same punishment she showed in martyring the saints.

> And a strong angel took up a stone as it were a great millstone and cast it into the sea, saying, thus with a mighty fall shall Babylon, the great city, be cast down, and shall be found no more at all.
>
> Verse twenty-one

A strong angel appears for the third time in this chapter and picks up a huge stone, one as big as a millstone, and throws it into the sea as a symbol of the sudden, swift, violent, total destruction of Babylon. The angel assures the world that Babylon will never again be seen.

> And the voice of harpers and minstrels and flute-players and trumpeters shall be heard no more at all in thee; and no craftsman, of whatsoever craft, shall be found any more at all in thee; and the voice of a mill shall be heard no more at all in thee; and the light of the lamp shall shine no more at all in thee; and the voice of the bridegroom and of the bride shall be

heard no more at all in thee: for thy merchants were the princes of the earth; for with thy sorcery were all the nations deceived.

Verses twenty-two to twenty-three

Nevermore will all the things mentioned in verses twelve through fourteen be found again. The voices of harpers, minstrels, flute players, and trumpeters. No more craftsmen, no more sound of a mill grinding, no light emanating, no more weddings.

All of these will be a testament to her total destruction. She will vanish from the face of the earth forever.

The enormity of the sin of this religious system is once more mentioned in the closing verses of this chapter. First, her merchants will not only be held responsible for exporting their products worldwide but also for spreading the diabolical religious system worldwide.

Second, Babylon will use fake magical arts to deceive all nations during the Tribulation period to lure people into an immoral spiritual relationship with herself.

"And in her was found the blood of prophets and of saints, and of all that have been slain upon the earth" (verse twenty-four).

A third reason for Babylon's destruction is that she will be responsible for the martyrdom of prophets and saints. Her hatred for true believers will be transmitted worldwide as she inspires governments to kill believers.

Politically, Babylon symbolizes prideful rebellion against God. Religiously, Babylon symbolizes the origin of idolatrous religions and worship that has affected every nation down through time, with their satanic dogma and practices.

Economically, Babylon symbolizes the pride of wealth and sensuality, the worship of money, power, prosperity, and the spirit of covetous commercialism that dominates worldwide commerce. All of this will be destroyed, and *Babylon shall be found no more.*

Chapter Nineteen

After these things I heard as it were a great voice of a great multitude in heaven saying, Hallelujah; Salvation, and glory, and power, belong to our God: for true and righteous are his judgments; for he hath judged the great harlot, her that corrupted the earth with her fornication, and he hath avenged the blood of his servants at her hand. And a second time they say, Hallelujah. And her smoke goeth up for ever and ever. And the four and twenty elders and the four living creatures fell down and worshiped God that sitteth on the throne, saying, Amen; Hallelujah. And a voice came forth from the throne, saying, Give praise to our God, all ye his servants, ye that fear him, the small and the great.

Verses one to five

In stark contrast to the whining and crying of Babylon's associates, the heavenly beings burst forth with the worship service of praise to God. In these first five verses, we hear four shouts of praise for the fall of Babylon. These are four hallelujahs: for salvation, for divine justice, for worship, and for God's sovereignty.

The first hallelujah comes to signify that the final stage of God's redemptive plan has been fully activated, and the heavenly host responds accordingly. They praise God for deliverance over the beast, Babylon, and the antichrist. This takes place just before Jesus Christ comes back to take over the earth.

The word "hallelujah" means "praise the Lord!" The theme of salvation is shown in the book of Revelation in conjunction with victory and divine justice. God has indeed vindicated the injustice inflicted on His servants by dishing out true justice on the great prostitute, Babylon. She deserves the sentence because she has corrupted the earth and killed the saints of God.

This includes the martyred people of Revelation 6:10, who asked how long it would be before they would be avenged. The time has come for their question to be answered.

The second hallelujah adds to the first. Babylon's permanent end is celebrated in words reminiscent of the judgment of ancient Babylon in Isaiah 34:10 (KJV): "The smoke thereof shall go up forever; from generation to generation it shall lie waste; none shall pass through it forever and ever."

Political Babylon, *whose sins have reached unto heaven*, will be judged by God who has *remembered her iniquities* (Revelation 18:5). Therefore, the hosts of heaven will rejoice at her destruction and revel in anticipation of the final disposition of the antichrist, his prophet, and Satan who brought on this anti-God conspiracy.

"And I heard as it were the voice of a great multitude, and as the voice of many waters, and as the voice of mighty thunders, saying, Hallelujah: for the Lord our God, the Almighty, reigneth" (verse six).

This is the same great multitude that we saw back in chapter seven, the same voice of mighty waters and the same voice of mighty thunders. They join together and praise God for His retribution. The sound will be deafening as their praise echoes through the air.

"Let us rejoice and be exceeding glad, and let us give the glory unto him: for the marriage of the Lamb is come, and his wife hath made herself ready" (verse seven).

In addition, they encourage each other to celebrate and praise God, for the time has come for the marriage of Jesus and His church (who are now completely cleansed from all sins and from all corruption).

"And it was given unto her that she should array herself in fine linen, bright and pure: for the fine linen is the righteous acts of the saints" (verse eight).

The marriage of the Lamb is patterned after the Jewish marriage customs of biblical times. The marriage is separated into several steps. The first is matchmaking. The fathers of the bride and groom meet and arrange for the marriage. They agree on a dowry for the bride, which is paid to the father of the bride.

The next step is the betrothal. This phase normally was one year or longer. During this time, the bride was observed for her purity and would gather and prepare the necessary items for setting up her household. The groom would prepare living quarters for his new bride, usually attached to his father's house. That completion of these quarters was overseen by the groom's father. When the father deemed the quarters complete and ready for the next step, he would give his son permission to proceed.

On the day of the wedding, known only to the father of the groom and the groom himself, the groom would leave his father's house, gather up his friends, and lead a bridal procession to collect his bride. She would not know when he was coming and had to be ready at all times. The groom would arrive at the bride's home, take her from home, and lead the procession back to his newly prepared quarters.

Once back at their new home, the wedding ceremony would take place. Only the immediate families and two witnesses were invited to observe the ceremony. After the wedding came a marriage supper that was a week of feasting. After the marriage supper, the newly married couple would settle into their new home.

Please note: verse seven refers to the church as the wife of the Lamb. This tells us that the wedding has already taken place, and the wedding is moving now to the time of the wedding supper.

Only the closest friends of the new couple are invited to the wedding supper. They consider themselves to be especially honored to have been invited.

"And he saith unto me, Write, Blessed are they that are bidden to the marriage supper of the Lamb. And he saith unto me, These are the true words of God" (verse nine).

Now comes a question! Who are these blessed ones that are invited to the marriage supper of the Lamb? First, the Lamb is the Lord Jesus Christ. The bride is the church. The New Testament pictures the church as a betrothed virgin waiting for the

Groom to return from His Father's house, where He has been preparing a dwelling place for her.

> In my Father's house are many mansions; if it were not so, I would have told you; for I go to prepare a place for you. And if I go and prepare a place for you, I come again, and will receive you unto myself; that where I am, there you may be also.
>
> John 14:2–3

God made all of the arrangements for the purchase of Jesus' bride by paying the bride price, the blood of His Son. God is in the process of perfecting the church in order to present her as a chaste virgin to Jesus (2 Corinthians 11:2). She is now going through the process of sanctification by being *washed by the water of God's Word* (Ephesians 5:26). Complete and total sanctification will take place during the rapture of the church when believers are changed from corruptible to incorruptible.

Then, at the judgment seat of Christ, the bride, the glorious church, will be presented to Jesus Christ *without spot, wrinkle, or blemish* (Ephesians 5:27).

How will the church be dressed? She will be *arrayed in fine linen*, clean and white, for the righteousness of the saints. This is not the righteousness obtained at salvation, but Christ's righteousness produced in the inner life and charter of believers.

Fine linen represents the righteous deeds of godliness produced by the Holy Spirit. These are the believers' good works that are to bring glory and honor to Christ's name. We will stand before Jesus clothed in whatever righteous acts remain after our works have been tested by fire (1 Corinthians 3:10–15). While we wait for Jesus' return, we are weaving the wedding garments that will clothe us at the wedding supper.

Next, the wedding supper is to be held at the Father's house, or in heaven. This will take place after the judgment seat of Christ and during the Tribulation period. While God's wrath is being poured out on the earth, the church will first be judged as to how they lived their Christian lives and then rewarded for their works, after which the church will be united with Jesus Christ forever.

"And from the time that the continual burnt-offering shall be taken away, and the abomination that maketh desolate set up, there shall be a thousand and two hundred and ninety days" (Daniel 12:11).

This is the proof text that tells us that the sacrificial offering system that was reinstated at the beginning of the Tribulation period will end 1,290 days into the seven-year period, or exactly in the middle of the Tribulation period.

"Blessed is he that waiteth, and cometh to the thousand three hundred and thirty days" (Daniel 12:12).

After the 1,290 days of the second half of the Tribulation, this period will come to an end. The wedding supper comes forty-five days after the Tribulation period has ended (Daniel 12:11–12) and Jesus has returned.

The guest list will be composed of Old Testament saints and those righteous men martyred during the Tribulation period. A good example of the guests who will be there is John the Baptist. He did not consider himself as the bridegroom or a part of the bride but only a friend of the Bridegroom.

Ye yourselves bear me witness, that I said, I am not the Christ, but, that I am sent before him. He hath the bride is the bridegroom: but the friend of the bridegroom, that standeth and heareth him, rejoiceth greatly because of the bridegroom's voice: this my joy therefore is made full.

John 3:28–29

John the Baptist, then the friend of the Bridegroom, will be among the honored guests who will rejoice at the wedding between Jesus Christ and His church.

And I fell down before his feet to worship him. And he saith unto me, See thou do it not: I am a fellow servant with thy brethren that hold the testimony of Jesus: worship God; for the testimony of Jesus is the spirit of prophecy.

Verse ten

John was so smitten with the angel's revelation that he fell down at the angel's feet to worship him, but he rebuked John and revealed that he and the righteous angels are but God's slaves, along with all righteous men of all times and all Christians.

"And I saw the heaven opened; and behold, a white horse, and he that sat thereon called Faithful and True; and in righteousness he doth judge and make war" (verse eleven).

We now shift back to the earth! John sees heaven open up, and a rider comes from heaven riding a white horse and on His way to the earth. As you remember, a rider on a white horse is significant of a victorious military leader returning home after winning a decisive battle.

Note: this Rider comes from heaven. Back in chapter six, the rider of the white horse came from the earth. As we go through these verses, note the differences between the two riders.

First, look at the emphasis on Jesus' names. He is said to be faithful and true. This is in contrast to the beast who was unfaithful and broke the covenant with Israel and true in contrast with the beast who ruled by means of deception and idolatry.

In the attribute of God, which is perfect righteousness, Jesus comes to judge the wicked and their leaders and make war against them.

"And his eyes are a flame of fire, and upon his head are many diadems; and he hath a name written which no one knoweth but himself" (verse twelve).

The greatness of Jesus' names is not the only quality we see in Him. Here we see His eyes shining forth like blazing bolts of lightning. His piercing gaze will reveal the hearts of all that He sees, and as the wickedness of those who dwell on the earth is revealed, He will bring judgment on them.

"And he is arrayed in a garment sprinkled with blood: and his name is called the Word of God" (verse thirteen).

Jesus will be wearing clothing that is soaked with blood, but it is not His blood, but the blood of His enemies. This Rider is further identified here as the Word of God. This is the name of Jesus that John speaks of in the first several verses of the Gospel according to John:

In the beginning was the Word, and the Word was
with God, and the Word was God. The Same was in
the beginning with God. All things were made by
Him, and without Him was not any thing made that
was made. [...] And the Word was made of flesh and
dwelt among us, (and we beheld His glory, the glory
as of the only begotten of the Father,) full of grace and
truth.

John 1:1–2, 14 (KJV)

"And the armies which are in heaven followed him upon
white horses, clothed in fine linen, white and pure" (verse
fourteen).

As Jesus appears from out of heaven, a huge army follows
Him, also riding white horses. They are clothed in the finest of
linen, which is brilliant white.

This army is composed of the Lamb's wife, the glorified
church. The fine, white linen identifies this army as the righteous, glorified church.

And out of his mouth precedeth a sharp sword, that
with it he should smite the nations: and he shall rule
them with a rod of iron: and he treadeth the winepress
of the fierceness of the wrath of God, the Almighty.

Verse fifteen

The sharp sword going out of his mouth is the same sharp
sword we saw in the description of the Son of Man in Revela-

tion 1:16, then in His letter to the church in Pergamum, in His exhortation to them in Revelation 2:12, 16. These were warnings to that church that unless they repented, they would meet the same destiny as the unsaved nations. In the first case, the warning was remedial. Here, there is no warning and is strictly execution of His punishment.

The rod is a tool of a shepherd. It is a tool for correction. But to rule with a rod of iron indicates severity, and in the context of this chapter, means to destroy.

When grapes ripened, they were put into a trough and pressed until the juice flowed into a vat. If the grapes were tried into excess, the vat would overflow. In Revelation 14:19, it says, "And the angel cast his sickle into the earth, and gathered the vintage of the earth, and cast it into the winepress, the great winepress, of the wrath of God." This is when Jesus will defeat the mighty army of Satan in battle when the blood runs as deep as a horse's bridle in the valley of Jehoshaphat (Joel 3:14).

All of the fury of God's wrath will pour itself out in heated anger on His enemies in this great, final battle of the Tribulation period. It will be unbelievably fierce!

"And he hath on his garment and on his thigh a name written, KING OF KINGS, AND LORD OF LORDS" (verse sixteen).

In this verse, we see the identification of the Rider of the white horse and no uncertain terms. He is the King of kings and Lord of lords. It is as King of kings that Jesus treads the winepress. In doing this, He proves the testimony of Isaiah 63:3:

> I have trodden the winepress alone; And of the peoples there was no man with me: yea, I trod them in

mine anger, and trampled them in my wrath; And their lifeblood is sprinkled upon my garments, and I have stained all my raiment.

This also refers back to verse thirteen, where He speaks of His garment dipped in blood.

"And I saw an angel standing in the sun; And he cried with a loud voice, saying to all the birds that fly in mid heaven, Come and be gathered together unto the great supper of God" (verse seventeen).

It seems incomprehensible that an angel can stand in the sun. However, God's Word says he is doing so! Even when something seems impossible, faith in God and His written Word makes the impossible possible. And this angel stands there, making an announcement to the whole world: it is an invitation to the carrion-eating birds to come and gorge themselves on the body of God's fallen enemies. He has prepared for them a great feast.

That ye may eat the flesh of kings, and the flesh of captains, and the flesh of mighty men, and the flesh of horses and of them that sit thereon, and the flesh of all men, both free and bond, and small and great.

Verse eighteen

Their menu is the same as listed in Ezekiel 39:18–20:

Ye shall eat the flesh of the mighty, and drink the blood of the princes of the earth, of rams, of lambs, and of goats, of bullocks, all of them fatlings of Bashan. And ye shall eat fat till ye be full, and drink blood till ye be drunken, of my sacrifice which I have sacrificed for you. And ye shall be filled at my table with horses and chariots, with mighty men, and with all men of war, saith the Lord Jehovah.

Of interest is how many prophecies are fulfilled in this chapter. It doesn't matter what level of society or government a person may belong to; if they reject Jesus as Savior, they will end up as food for the buzzards.

"And I saw the beast, and the kings of the earth, and their armies, gathered together to make war against him that sat upon the horse, and against his army" (verse nineteen).

This is the final battle of the Tribulation period, which is called *the battle of Armageddon* (Revelation 16:13–16). All of the evil and demonic beings and men gather together to engage Jesus in a winner-take-all fight.

And the beast was taken, and with him the false prophet that wrought the signs in his sight, wherewith he deceived them that had received the mark of the beast and them that worshiped his image: they two were cast alive into the lake of fire that burneth with brimstone.

Verse twenty

Immediately at the start of this battle, the beast and false prophet were captured by Jesus and thrown, while still alive, into the lake of fire. This lake is seen only in the book of Revelation! It is defined as a place of fiery everlasting torment prepared for the devil and his followers.

It is fitting that those two demonic leaders will be alone in the lake of fire for 1,000 years before anyone else will go there. Not only will they be alone there, but the fact that they were thrown in alive indicates that their suffering will be worse than the rest of the damned. Added to that is that everyone thrown into this lake will be in a conscious existence forever!

Note: the lake of fire is *not* the same as hell! We will see later that hell is a temporary holding place for the wicked until the Great White Throne Judgment. Hell is a picnic compared to the lake of fire.

"And the rest were killed with the sword of him that sat upon the horse, even the sword which came forth out of his mouth: and all the birds were filled with their flesh" (verse twenty-one).

After the beast and false prophet have been thrown into the lake of fire, the remainder of the evil army will be totally destroyed. Every single person in this army will be killed. Jesus will kill them all with the sword of the Lord, the Word of God, which will be spoken out.

Just as Jesus spoke the world into existence, He will speak these evil men out of physical existence. They will all die, and the birds that were invited to a feast will come and gorge themselves with the remains of the devil's army.

As we will see in the next chapter, of all of those who were alive on the earth, not a single one will remain. The only evil personage who remains is Satan, and we will see what happens to him in this next chapter.

Chapter Twenty

After the destruction of the beast, his prophet, and their followers, Satan is dealt with.

"And I saw an angel coming down out of heaven, having the key of the abyss and a great chain in his hand" (verse one).

We have seen two previous mentions of an angel coming down out of heaven: Revelation 10:1 and 18:1. In both of these incidences, details of the extreme importance of the mission of each angel were revealed. This angel carried the key to the abyss. This is the same abyss that we saw in Revelation 9:1–2, which the star from heaven opened to release the demonic locusts.

The angel was carrying a *great chain* with him.

"And he laid hold on the dragon, the old serpent, which is the Devil and Satan, and bound him for a thousand years" (verse two).

The angel takes hold of Satan and binds him for one thousand years. This is the first place in Scripture where a spirit being is said to be bound, even though the King James Version of 2 Peter 2:4 says that *the fallen angels were cast down to hell and bound in chains*. In Greek, it says something different and, if translated, will be: "For if God spared not the sinning angels, but delivered them to Tartarus and consigned them in pits of gloom where they were kept until the judgment."

Tartarus is a special place that God created for the fallen spirit beings. It is a separate place from all others and is below hell, deeper and more remote. From the context of the book of Revelation, so, too, is the abyss a special place.

Therefore, the fallen spirit beings, or fallen angels, or demons, will be confined in a place specially prepared for them until the time of judgment. Then they will be brought before the throne of God, where the church will judge them (1 Corinthians 6:3).

"And cast him into the abyss, and shut it, and sealed it over him, that he should deceive the nation's no more, until the thousand years should be finished: after this he must be loosed for a little time" (verse three).

The angel was given the power to handle the devil, and he restrained him with a chain from heaven and threw him into the abyss. The abyss will be sealed. The elaborate measures taken to ensure his custody are most easily understood when we consider that Satan will not be able to leave the abyss, nor will he be able to deceive humans. He will be in solitary confinement for the entire 1,000 years.

Remember this: the 1,000 years will be concurrent with the millennial-kingdom rule of Jesus Christ. It is at the end of the millennium when Satan will be let loose again, but only for a short time.

> And I saw thrones, and they sat upon them, and judgment was given unto them: and I saw the souls of

them that had been beheaded for the testimony of Jesus, and for the word of God, and such as worshiped not the beast, neither his image, and received not the mark upon their forehead and upon their hand; and they lived, and reigned with Christ a thousand years.

Verse four

We are given no information on life during the millennium. John only records who will participate in it. There is one thing to note here: Jesus Christ and His church will reign and rule over the nations of the earth. The church will sit on thrones and will judge the twelve tribes of Israel and also angels (Matthew 19:28, 1 Corinthians 6:3). Judgment is given only to this first group mentioned!

The second group of people recorded here are those who were martyred during the Tribulation period. Their entry into the millennium kingdom was brought by their testimony for Jesus, for which they were beheaded, for their faith in the Word of God, and for their refusal to worship the beast, take his mark, or worship his image. These too lived and reigned with Jesus for the 1,000 years of the millennium period.

The third group of people who will enter into the millennial kingdom are the Old Testament righteous who will be resurrected in order that they may participate in the kingdom as they were promised. They will live in the kingdom ruled by the Son of David, their Messiah.

There is also a fourth group of people who are not mentioned here but are included in the book of Matthew, which I will refer to when describing the events in this chapter of the book of Revelation. These are those who give aid and protection to the Jews during the Tribulation period.

> But when the son of man shall come in his glory, and all the angels with him, then shall he sit on the throne of his glory: and before him shall be gathered all the nations: and he shall separate them one from another, as the shepherd separateth the sheep from the goats; and he shall set the sheep on his right hand, but the goats on the left. Then shall the king say unto them on his right hand, Come, ye blessed of my Father, inherit the kingdom prepared for you from the foundation of the world: for I was hungry, and ye gave me to eat; I was thirsty, and ye gave me to drink; I was a stranger, and ye took me in; naked and ye clothed me; I was sick, and ye visited me; I was in prison, and ye came unto me. Then shall the righteous answer him, saying, Lord, when saw we thee hungry, and fed thee? or athirst, and gave thee drink? And when saw we thee a stranger, and took thee in? or naked, and clothed thee? and when saw we thee sick, or in prison, and came unto thee? And the King shall answer and say unto them, Verily I say unto you, inasmuch as ye did it unto one of these my brethren, even these least, ye did it for me.
>
> Matthew 25:31–40

"The rest of the dead lived not until the thousand years should be finished. This is the first resurrection" (verse five).

The rest of the dead are those wicked dead who will remain in hell until the end of the millennial reign of Jesus Christ is completed. They will then be resurrected.

The first resurrection refers to those who are righteous. This is in contrast to the last resurrection that will take place at the end of the millennium period. Daniel 12:2 says of this, "And many of them that sleep in the dust of the earth shall awake, some to everlasting life, and some to shame and everlasting contempt."

Those who are resurrected at the beginning of the millennium period will have eternal life, but those who are resurrected at the end of the millennial period will spend eternity in shame and contempt. We will see more of their destination later on in our study.

> Blessed and holy is he that hath part of the first resurrection: over these the second death hath no power; but they shall be priests of God and of Christ, and shall reign with him a thousand years.
>
> Verse six

Those who are righteous, blessed, and holy are those who are members of the family of God, who have been resurrected to enter into the millennial kingdom. Death will no longer be a consideration for them. In the millennium, they will become priests of God and Jesus Christ and will reign with Him.

> And when the thousand years are finished, Satan shall be loosed out of his prison, and shall come forth

to deceive the nations which are in the four corners of the earth, Gog and Magog, to gather them together to the war: the number of whom is as the sand of the sea.

Verse seven

After the thousand years have been completed, Satan will be turned loose from his confinement in the abyss. Why on earth will he be let loose? The answer is, so he can deceive the nations that are in the four corners of the earth. These people are those who were born during the millennium. Like us, they will be born with a sin nature inherited from Adam and will have to make a choice between Jesus or the devil. These are the descendants of Gog and Magog.

Even after 1,000 years with Jesus personally sitting on the throne of the world, ruling honestly, justly, and perfectly, there will be people who will reject Him. This fact is attributed to the deep, complex source of rebellion that emanates from evil. All the time the devil is chained, mankind will act perfectly. Once he has the freedom to lie again, his evil will fog man's brains and cause them to sin. It will be "Adam and Eve" all over again. The return of Satan will prove this in a dramatic way.

In Ezekiel, chapters thirty-nine and forty, Gog is referred to as the prince of a host of pagan invaders from the north, and Magog as Scythians. Scythia is a region in Asia and Southern Europe. The descendants of Gog and Magog are those who will rebel against Jesus after hearing Satan's lies.

Satan will talk them into rebelling against Jesus, and there will be so many deceived that they will be numbered as the grains of sand on the seashore.

"And they went up over the breadth of the earth, and compassed the camp of the saints about, and the beloved city: and fire came down out of heaven, and devoured them" (verse nine).

There are only two cities mentioned in the book of Revelation, Babylon and Jerusalem. The city of the harlot, which is Babylon, and the city of God, which is Jerusalem. This huge army will encircle Jerusalem. Within seconds, fire comes down from heaven and totally destroys the entire army.

"And the devil that deceived them was cast into the lake of fire and brimstone, where are also the beast and the false prophet; and they shall be tormented day and night for ever and ever" (verse ten).

The age-long leader and author of sin who has deceived mankind for thousands of years now meets his final defeat. Jesus casts him into the lake of fire where the beast and false prophet have been suffering for 1,000 years. Together, these three members of the false trinity will be tormented day and night for eternity, never again to be released or have the privilege of being with God. This eternal judgment shows the permanency of God's judgment.

"And I saw a great white throne, and him that sat up on it, from whose face the earth and heaven fled away; and there was found no place for them" (verse eleven).

John now will describe in vivid pictures the final judgment of unrepentant mankind. Unlike the paintings of old we have seen based on this verse of Scripture, John describes an unearthly scene. God is sitting on his great white throne. Heaven and the earth have disappeared. There is no longer a reason for their existence. All of creation has now moved into the eternal state and will no longer require a special environment that has been prepared for their existence. That is, all living beings will be transformed from our corruptible existence to incorruptible. We will not need air to breathe, food to eat, liquids to drink, houses to live in, or clothing to wear.

> And I saw the dead, the great and small, standing before the throne; and books were opened: and another book was opened, which is the book of life: and the dead were judged out of the things which were written in the books, according to their works.
>
> Verse twelve

These dead ones are those written of in verse five who live not again until the 1,000 years are finished. These are all of the wicked, unrepentant, ungodly people since Adam and Eve. These are those whose destination is shame and everlasting contempt (Daniel 12:2), the resurrection of judgment (John 5:29), and the resurrection of the unjust (Acts 24:15).

These have been held in hell since their deaths. They will be resurrected and stand before the throne of God, where they will be judged by the almighty God. To ensure there is no one before the throne who shouldn't be there, the ledgers that contain the records of each person's life will be opened. Notice the wording: books will be opened. While there is only one book of life, there will be many books containing the records of the wicked. Every evil and wicked act done by those whose names are in these books will become public. Not one sin will be left out.

God will then judge each person according to their works. That is, God is fair and just, and being so, He will give penalties to each person according to the degree of their sins. As an example, gossip will not be as serious as murder, but both will receive a degree of punishment. What this degree of punishment will be is not written.

After confronting each of these with their sins, God will turn to the book of life and check to make sure none of their names are written within. The significance of the book of life is that if a name is not written in this book, there can be no objection to God's punishment, for everyone in history has had an opportunity to come to God. This particular group of people are those who made the wrong choice. They rejected God, and in doing so, rejected eternal life!

"And the sea gave up the dead that were in it; and death and Hades gave up the dead that were in them: and they were judged every man according to their works" (verse thirteen).

A special reference is made to those who lost their lives by drowning and those who were buried at sea. This is to show that resurrection is normally spoken of as coming up out of the grave. This also shows that no matter where the body of a dead one is buried, the body will be resurrected and return to its original form. This would include those who lost body parts or were completely blown apart. God is able to collect every atom of every body and put them back together again.

Death and Hades, or hell, are written here as if they are inseparable, and so they are called on to give up the dead that they are holding. The people held by the companions, death and Hades, are brought before the Great White Throne of God to stand trial for the deeds done in their lifetime and receive the sentencing for their sins, every man according to their works.

"And death and Hades were cast into the lake of fire. This is the second death, even the lake of fire" (verse fourteen).

There will also then be no further need for death and Hades. From this point on, there will be no more sin, so there will no longer be a need for death or a place of punishment for unrepentant sinners, so hell will no longer be needed. Therefore, both death and hell will be burned up in the lake of fire, which is the place of the second death.

"And if any was not found written in the book of life, he was cast into the lake of fire" (verse fifteen).

A search of the list of the names in the book of life will be made, and if any of those who are standing before the throne of God does not have his or her name written in this book, he or she will be immediately thrown into the Lake of Fire to join the beast, the false prophet, Satan, and his or her fellow unrepentant sinners. This implies that not even a trace of their name was found! There is no appeal!

They have just been sentenced to the second death, which is eternal damnation and punishment. Through eternity, these people will experience all the neglected opportunities they had to repent of and will know they have only themselves to blame.

This will be the end of human history on the earth.

Chapter Twenty-One

"And I saw a new heaven and a new earth: for the first heaven and the first earth are passed away; and the sea is no more" (verse one).

Chapter twenty-one begins a new history of God's people. As he begins this chapter, John records that he sees a brand-new heaven and earth. The old heaven and earth are no longer in existence. Even the sea has disappeared. Everything is brand-new!

The book of Revelation does not record what happened to old heaven and earth, so we will have to look elsewhere for that information. We find it in 2 Peter 3:10–13:

> But the day of the Lord will come as a thief; in the which the heavens shall pass away with a great noise, and the elements shall be dissolved with fervent heat, and the earth and the works that are therein shall be burned up. Seeing that these things are thus all to be dissolved, what manner of persons ought ye to be an all holy living and godliness, looking for and earnestly desiring the coming of the day of God, by reason of which the heavens being on fire shall be dissolved,

and the elements shall melt with fervent heat? But according to his promise, we look for new heavens and a new earth, wherein dwelleth righteousness.

This passage in 2 Peter is more graphic than here in the book of Revelation, but nonetheless, both tell us that the earth as we now know it will be completely destroyed, and not a trace of it will be left. Peter goes on to say, "According to God's promise, we look for new heavens and a new earth. On this new earth, there will be only righteousness. Sin will forever be gone!"

"And I saw the holy city, new Jerusalem, coming down out of heaven from God, made ready as a bride adorned for her husband" (verse two).

Jerusalem has always been called the holy city (except in Revelation 11:2: after the Gentiles trod down the city, it is called Sodom). But the city is also melted in fervent heat when the heavens and the earth are dissolved.

But God will build a new Jerusalem in heaven. When human history is completed and eternity begins for us, this new Jerusalem will descend in all of its glory, ready for God's people to live in. We see the Jewish wedding influence in the way God sees His people. Just as the church is the bride of Christ and Israel is the wife of God, all humans are considered to be the love of God.

Of note is how God is named. We do not see Jesus separated from the Godhead now. We see the triune God all in all. Yet, we will still be able to see Jesus as He is, that is in human form, with His nail-scarred hands, for eternity. He is our Lord, our Savior, our eternal God.

And I heard a great voice out of the throne saying, Behold, the tabernacle of God is with men, and he shall dwell with them, and they shall be his peoples, and God himself shall be with them, and be their God.

Verse three

This is the last time we will see this notation of a great voice coming from out of the throne (there have been twenty-one such voices). This voice informs us that the tabernacle of God is again with men. There has been no tabernacle (or Temple) since AD 70 when the Temple was destroyed by the Romans (except for the first three and a half years of the Tribulation period). And even then, the Shechinah glory of God was not present, nor has it been present since leaving the Temple because of Israel's idolatry and going up from the city of Jerusalem and then ascending from the Mount of Olives (Ezekiel 8–11).

But in the new Jerusalem, on the new earth, God will once more be present with men, and His presence will be permanent. That what God and man have longed for will finally become a reality.

"And he shall wipe away every teardrop from their eyes; and death shall be no more; neither shall there be mourning, nor crying, nor pain, anymore: the first things are passed away" (verse four).

Since the day Adam and Eve sinned in the Garden of Eden, tears, toil, sweat, heartache, wars, pain, the curse of childbirth, and death have been man's lot. In the new Jerusalem, all of this will be gone. The curse caused by sin will be gone. The problems of fragile bodies will be over. God and man will live in fellowship forever in the new Jerusalem.

"And he that sitteth on the throne said, Behold, I will make all things new. And he saith, Write: for these words are faithful and true" (verse five).

Once more, we see the singular He who is sitting on the throne. Again, this is the triune God: Father, Son, and Holy Spirit, who announces to John: the new heaven, the new earth, the new Jerusalem are all included in His statement. There will be nothing left of the old universe. Everything will be made new. Everything!

Evidently, John was so taken aback by observing all that was happening in his vision that he had stopped writing, for God gives him the command, "Write!" and then He confirms that everything John has witnessed is faithful and true.

"And he said unto me, They are come to pass. I am the Alpha and the Omega, the beginning and the end. I will give unto him that is athirst of the fountain of the water of life freely" (verse six).

God reiterates that everything John has seen will become a reality. It will become past history. He then tells John that He, God, is the originator of everything and that at a particular point in time (Greek: *telos*), everything will reach its limit. The first thing that God created was time. Here we see Him conveying to John that He will end that created time.

After all the scenes of judgment and outpouring of His wrath, God once again offers the water of life, that is, eternal life, to anyone that desires it.

"He that overcometh shall inherit these things; and I will be his God, and he shall be my son" (verse seven).

There are many promises pertaining to what the faithful will inherit: the earth, everlasting life, the kingdom, and other promises, but here God promises all things. But in order to overcome, a person must come to Christ. He is the only way to eternal life.

> But for the fearful, and unbelieving, and abominable, and murderers, and fornicators, and sorcerers, and idolaters, and all liars, their part shall be in the lake that burneth with fire and brimstone; which is the second death.
>
> Verse eight

Now comes the qualifier: but! This is the first of three lists of the wicked reported in the last two chapters of the book of Revelation. The other two are in Revelation 21:27 and 22:15. For convenience and comparison, they are shown as follows:

21:8: fearful, unbelieving, abominable, murderers, whoremongers, sorcerers, idolaters, and all liars;

21:27: all who defile, all who work abomination, and all who make a lie;

22:15: dogs—sorcerers, horror mongers, murderers, idolaters, and all who love a lie and all who lie.

This is a total of thirteen different categories of sins. Liars the biggest group of all? Isn't it interesting to know that God lists liars as being worse than a murderer? Sorcerers, whoremongers, murderers, and idolaters are mentioned twice. Nevertheless, all of these have a destination, which is to be thrown into the lake of fire.

And there came one of the seven angels who had
the seven bowls, who were laden with the seven last
plagues; and he spake with me, saying, Come hither,
I will show the bride, the wife of the Lamb.

Verse nine

One of the angels who had carried one of the bowls containing God's wrath came to John and told him to follow him. He
had something to show John. He would show him the bride, the
wife of the Lamb, now eternally joined with Him.

"And he carried me away in the Spirit to a mountain great
and high, and showed me the holy city Jerusalem, coming down
out of heaven from God" (verse ten).

John was then transported to a great, high mountain. He
was in the spirit (that is, he saw all this in his vision), and he
was shown the holy city of the new Jerusalem as it descended
from God in heaven.

"Having the glory of God: her light was like unto a stone
most precious, as it were a jasper stone, clear as crystal" (verse
eleven).

The new Jerusalem is alit with the *Shechinah* glory of God!
This light comes from the radiance of God Himself. The light is
reflected like sunlight shining through a diamond. Every facet
emits a different color, like precious gemstones.

"Having a wall great and high; having twelve gates, and at
the gates twelve angels; and the names are written thereon,
which are the names of the twelve tribes of the children of Israel" (verse twelve).

The new Jerusalem will be encircled by a very high wall. Inset into the wall are twelve gates. Each gate is guarded by an angel, and each gate has the name of one of the twelve tribes of Israel.

"On the east were three gates; and on the north three gates; and on the south three gates; and on the west three gates" (verse thirteen).

Three gates are located on each side of the city and face the four points of the compass: east, north, south, and west.

If the arrangement of the tribes follows the example shown in Ezekiel 48:31–34, the order will be as follows: on the east: Joseph, Benjamin, Dan. On the north: Ruben, Judah, Levi. On the south: Simeon, Issachar, Zebulun. On the west: Gad, Asher, Neftali.

"And the wall of the city had twelve foundations, and on them twelve names of the twelve apostles of the Lamb" (verse fourteen).

The wall had twelve gates named after the twelve tribes of Israel, and now we see that the wall also has twelve foundations. These twelve foundations are named after the New Testament apostles of the Lamb, Jesus Christ. Unlike the possible positions of the twelve tribes on each side of the city, there is no order of placement of the names of the twelve apostles in relation to the twelve foundations.

However, we do know their names: Peter, Andrew, James, John, Phillip, Bartholomew, Matthew, Thomas, James—son of Alphaeus, Thaddeus, Simon, and Mathias (who replaced Judas Iscariot).

"And he that spake with me had for a measure a golden reed to measure the city, and the gates thereof, and the wall thereof" (verse fifteen).

The angel who was speaking to John was carrying a golden reed, which was used for measuring. We saw back in Revelation 11:1 that a reed was used as a measuring device, and in Ezekiel 40:5 that a reed is six cubits long, or nine feet. This reed was made of gold.

> And the city lieth foursquare, and the length thereof is as great as the breadth: and he measured the city with the reed, twelve thousand furlongs: the length and breadth and the height thereof are equal.
>
> Verse sixteen

Here we see that the city is laid out in a square. Each side of the city measures 12,000 stadia, or approximately 1,400 miles. The walls were also the same height as the walls were long. This is equal to the distance from northern Maine to Key West, Florida, and from the East Coast to beyond the Mississippi River. This is going to be one huge city!

It is said that if you were to put every living human being on the earth today in Texas, you wouldn't fill the state. I forget how many square feet it was forwarded, but even if these people were standing shoulder to shoulder and Texas would hold them, how many could a city of 1,400 miles square and 1,400 miles high contain? Consider this also: the city could have multiple levels!

"And he measured the wall thereof, a hundred and forty and four cubits, according to the measure of a man, that is, of an angel" (verse seventeen).

The walls are 144 cubits thick, or approximately 200 feet thick. In Scripture, angels always are depicted as being in the form of a man. Therefore, the dimensions of the city are based on man's size, that is, cubits, or the length of the forearm from the fingertips to the elbow, which averages to be about eighteen inches. So, the angels' measurements are the same.

"And the building of the wall thereof was jasper: and the city was pure gold, like unto pure glass" (verse eighteen).

Jasper is an opaque quartz mineral and occurs in a number of colors. It is commonly red, brown, green, and yellow. In bright light, jasper changes colors, so these walls will constantly shimmer in different colors, reflecting the glory of God.

The city itself is constructed of pure gold. Man has never seen such purity. This gold is so pure that it is as transparent as glass.

"The foundations of the wall of the city were adorned with all manner of precious stones. The first foundation was jasper; the second, sapphire; the third, chalcedony; the fourth, emerald" (verse nineteen).

Each of the twelve foundations of the wall of the city is decorated with precious gemstones. Each foundation is decorated with a different type of gem. The first is decorated with jasper. As described earlier, jasper is a reddish, brown or yellow, opaque variety of quartz. The second is decorated with sapphires. Sapphire is a relatively pure form of corundum, usually blue in color. Chalcedony is a transparent milky quartz with crystals arranged in parallel bands. And emeralds are light green.

"The fifth, sardonyx; the sixth, sardius; the seventh, chrysolite; the eighth beryl; the ninth, topaz; the tenth, chrysoprase; the eleventh jacinth; the twelfth amethyst" (verse twenty).

The fifth foundation was decorated with sardonyx. Sardonyx is a type of onyx with alternating bands of white and brown. Sardius, a variety of chalcedony, decorated the sixth foundation. The seventh was decorated with chrysolite, a golden yellow crystal. The eighth was adorned with beryl. Beryl is a silicate gemstone that is a bluish-green color. The ninth foundation was decorated with topaz. Topaz is a light yellow variety of quartz. The tenth foundation was decorated with chrysoprase. Chrysoprase is an apple-green type of chalcedony. The eleventh was decorated with jacinth. Jacinth is a reddish-orange variety of zircon. The twelfth foundation was ornamented with amethyst, which are violet or purple gemstones.

"And the twelve gates were twelve pearls; each one of the several gates was one pearl: and the street of the city was pure gold, as it were transparent glass" (verse twenty-one).

Each of the twelve gates was made from individual pearls. Since the gate is approximately 20' to 30' wide and the same height, these are some giant pearls. Imagine how big the oysters who made them must be! And the streets will be paved with pure transparent gold.

To summarize: the new Jerusalem is going to be a huge city, constructed of pure transparent gold, foundations decorated with precious gems of every color of the rainbow, with gates each made from a single pearl, and streets also of pure transparent gold.

This will be some city!

"And I saw no temple therein: for the Lord God the Almighty, and the Lamb, are the temple thereof" (verse twenty-two).

A temple was designed to be a place to go and worship God. With God the Almighty and the Lamb always present, we will have no need for a temple. We will be in His presence and can worship Him in person anytime or all the time. He is the temple!

"And the city hath no need of the sun, neither of the moon, to shine upon it: for the glory of God did lighten it, and the lamp thereof is the Lamb" (verse twenty-three).

With the glory of God shining in all its brilliance, the sun and the moon would be insignificant. There will be no need for them in the new heaven and earth.

"And the nations shall walk amidst the light thereof: and the kings of the earth bring their glory into it" (verse twenty-four).

From the wording of this verse, it appears that there will be nations established outside the new Jerusalem. The areas where the nations are positioned will also be illuminated by the glory of God. Those who are given the positions of kings will come into the city to glorify God.

"And the gates thereof shall in no wise be shut by day (for there shall be no night there)" (verse twenty-five).

Since there is no night, the gates of the new Jerusalem will never be closed.

"And they shall bring the glory and the honor of the nations into it" (verse twenty-six).

Everyone will come to the new Jerusalem for the purpose of glorifying and honoring God.

Of note: the church, the wife of Jesus Christ, will be residents of the new Jerusalem. The Scriptures promise that wherever He is, the church will always be with Him for eternity.

"And there shall in no wise enter into anything unclean, or he that maketh an abomination and a lie: but only they that are written in the Lamb's book of life" (verse twenty-seven).

Nothing unclean will ever be seen or heard of in the new Jerusalem or in eternity. All sin has been eradicated, and only those who have been made righteous by the Lamb of God and have their names written in the Lamb's book of life will be there.

What we see here is the absolute purity of all who have access to the city. In God's eternity, there is only purity.

Chapter Twenty-Two

"And he showed me a river of water of life, bright as crystal, proceeding out of the throne of God and of the Lamb" (verse one).

In chapter twenty-two, we resume the description of the new Jerusalem, but now the angel shows John the inner details of the city. First, the angel shows John a river of crystal-pure water. The quality of this water is reminiscent of the purity of the water in the Garden of Eden.

The water issues forth from the throne of God and the Lamb. Since this entire city is the holiest place with God as its center, everything comes from Him. All life, and all necessities, will come from the throne of God.

> In the midst of the street thereof. And on this side of the river and on that was the tree of life, bearing twelve manner of fruits, yielding its fruit every month: and the leaves of the tree were for the healing of the nations.
>
> Verse two

This river flows down the middle of the street, which also emanates from the throne of God. There is a tree growing on both banks of the river. This tree is the tree of life. It is hard to imagine a single tree that is growing on both banks of a river, but the Greek text clearly states that this is one tree.

When Adam and Eve sinned, man was prohibited from eating of the tree of life, but in the eternal home, man will have access to the tree of life. What was forfeited by our forebears in Eden and denied to succeeding posterity is now fully restored. The imagery of abundant fruit and medicinal leaves is symbolic of the far-reaching effects of Jesus' sacrificial death for the redeemed community. The eternal life God gives to the redeemed will be perpetually available, will sustain, and will cure eternally every former sin. We must remember that in our eternal state, we will not need to eat. We can, but this is not necessary. Neither will there be sickness and death.

"And there shall be no curse any more: and the throne of God and of the Lamb shall be therein: and his servants shall serve him" (verse three).

The curse of man that was pronounced in the Garden of Eden has been removed. All of the resultant effects will be gone. The throne of God will be the focal point of eternity, and all His servants will serve only Him. The service of the priestly saints will be perpetual.

Here on the earth, we are handicapped by sin and weakness. When we are with God for eternity, all hindrances to service will be removed and our service to Him will be perfect. What will our service consist of? Scripture doesn't tell us, but whatever it will be, it is sufficient to know that we will be able to serve Him without interference.

"And they shall see his face; and his name shall be on their foreheads" (verse four).

Never before has man been able to look on the face of God and live. Since we will at this time be in our glorified, eternal, and incorrupt bodies and will be like Jesus, man will be able to look God in the face for the first time in history.

Every one of God's people will have His mark on their foreheads. The mark will be His name.

"And there shall be night no more; and they need no light of lamp, neither light of sun; For the Lord God shall give them light: and they shall reign forever and ever" (verse five).

Finally, John writes that there will be no sunshine, no lamps, no artificial light of any kind. None will be necessary because God will be the source of light. His Shekinah glory will be exposed forever, and we will be in His light forever. And we will be with Him in His eternity, which has no end.

> And he said unto me, These words are faithful and true: and the Lord, the God of the spirits of the prophets, sent his angels to show unto his servants the things which must shortly come to pass.
>
> Verse six

The language here is practically identical to the first words of the prologue (Revelation 1:1). The contents of this book are faithful, and they are true. God sent His angels to show us everything that will come to pass.

In God's time scheme, all of the things written in the book of Revelation will be the next things to happen in His plan. "Shortly come to pass" means that nothing will have to take place before the events begin to unfold.

"And behold, I come quickly. Blessed is he that keepeth the words of the prophecy of this book" (verse seven).

Jesus is coming back for His church, and when He comes for His own, it will unleash all of the events recorded in this book. As far as the church is concerned, we have been adequately warned of what we need to do. The rest is up to us! We need to follow the guidance Jesus has given us in the words of this book. If we do, we will be blessed!

"And I John am he that heard and saw these things. And when I heard and saw, I fell down to worship before the feet of the angel that showed me these things" (verse eight).

John was so awed by the total of the vision he had received that he fell on his face before the angel who had delivered the message to him. This was the second time he erred by worshipping an angel. The first time was in Revelation 19:10.

"And he saith unto me, See thou do it not: I am a fellow-servant with thee and with thy brethren the prophets, and with them that keep the words of this book: worship God" (verse nine).

Here, as before, John is chastised by the angel who refuses the honor John has given him and reprimands him. The angels, John, and all of the brothers and sisters in Christ, the prophets, and all the godly men of history who are faithful to God and live according to His Word all are equal in God's eyes. We all have functions in His eternal kingdom; the primary is to worship and glorify God.

"And he saith unto me, Seal not up the words of the prophecy of this book; for the time is at hand" (verse ten).

Daniel was told to seal up the words of his prophecy (Daniel 12:9) because they were for the time of the end. Now John is told the time is at hand and that he should not seal up the words of the prophecy of this book. "The time is at hand" means that there is nothing that needs to happen before the events in this book begin to happen. We say that events are imminent and that the next things to happen are in God's plan.

It is hoped that Bible-believing Christians will pay closer attention to the prophecy of this book because world events seem to be indicating that, indeed, the end time is near!

"He that is unrighteous, let him do unrighteousness still: and he that is filthy, let him be made filthy still" (verse eleven).

These words seem to say there is a fixed destination for the wicked. Throughout the prophecy of this book, men have repeatedly refused the pardon offered by Jesus. They scoff at Him, reject His sacrificial offer of eternal life with Him, and blaspheme His name. They drive the nails into their own coffins.

"And he that is righteous, let him do righteousness still: and he that is holy, let him be made holy still" (verse eleven, part b).

There are those who ask, "Is it worth it to live a godly life?" Jesus' answer here is, "Yes! It is worth it!" Knowing that we will dwell in the heavenly city should make a difference in our lives here and now. The assurance we have of eternal life should not lull us into complacency or carelessness but spur us to fulfill our spiritual duties.

"Behold, I come quickly; and my reward is with me, to render to each man according as his work is" (verse twelve).

Revelation 22: 13 I am the Alpha and the Omega, the
first and the last, the beginning and the end.

In addition, Jesus' return will be so rapid that men will not
have time to change their hearts. These verses clearly warn
us that our decisions based on these scriptures have eternal
consequences.

If Jesus judges each man, woman, and child, we must keep
in mind that He will bring rewards and judgment to each individual. Rewards will be in accordance with how well we use
that which God has given us for His service, and judgment will
come in the same way. We will also reap what we sow!

"I am the Alpha and the Omega, the first and the last, the
beginning and the end" (verse thirteen).

Once again, Jesus tells us that He is the eternal God. He is
the Beginning (Alpha), and He is the End (Omega). He created
man's history, and He will end it as we know it.

294

"Blessed are they that wash their robes, that they may have the right to come to the tree of life, and may enter in by the gates into the city" (verse fourteen).

This is addressed to every person born into the world. The entry into the eternal city is allowed only to righteous men. Only the righteous will have eternal life.

"Without are the dogs, and the sorcerers, and the fornicators, and the murderers, and the idolaters come and everyone that loveth and maketh a lie" (verse fifteen).

All those who are unrighteous will be eternally outside the light of God. They will exist forever but will be in total darkness and eternal torment.

"I Jesus have sent mine angel to testify unto you these things for the churches. I am the root and the offspring of David, the bright, the morning star" (verse sixteen).

There should be a comma between the words "I" and "Jesus." This is the only time that "I, Jesus" has been used in the Scriptures, emphasizing the importance of this verse. Jesus is telling us that He, personally, has sent His angel specifically to the churches to bring His testimony of what will happen in the future. He hereby authenticates everything written in this book.

Any method of interpretation that blunts the application of this message is disregarding the words of Christ.

He is the Messiah of Israel, from the lineage of David (as prophesied), and He is the bright and morning Star.

When we get up from bed early and look into the sky, we see the morning star. The heavenly body we call the morning star is Venus. This *morning star* announces Jesus' arrival. He will come for His church as the morning Star. But when He comes to judge, it will be as the *Sun of Righteousness* and burning fury (Malachi 4:1–3).

"And the spirit and the bride say, Come. And he that heareth, let him say, Come. And he that is athirst, let him come: he that will, let him take the water of life freely" (verse seventeen).

Jesus has delayed His coming for 2,000 years. This verse, along with 2 Peter 3:1, tells us that God wants to give the sinful world opportunity to repent and be saved.

In the meantime, the Spirit of God and the church (the bride) call for man to come to Jesus and receive salvation. The invitation to come to Jesus is open to all who hear. It is a matter of individual choice.

It is also a matter of obedience of those in the church of Jesus Christ to witness for our Lord. It is up to us to invite those who are lost and who are spiritually thirsty to come and drink of the living water of Jesus Christ.

If the church is living in expectation of Jesus' return, this attitude will provoke evangelism and personal ministry, as well as produce purity of heart. We should eagerly desire to tell others of the grace of God and share His invitation of salvation to a lost world.

"I testify unto every man that heareth the words of the prophecy of this book, if any man shall add unto them, God shall add unto him the plagues which are written in this book" (verse eighteen).

Jesus dictates a final warning to those who are privy to the words written in the book of Revelation: "Do not add anything to this book!" This is not the first admonition to abstain from adding to Scripture. In John 10:35, Jesus says, "The scripture cannot be broken"; in Deuteronomy 4:2, it says, "Ye shall not add unto the word which I command you, neither shall ye diminish from it"; in Proverbs 30:5–6, it says, "Every word of God is tried: He is a shield unto them that take refuge in him. And thou not unto his words, Lest he reproved thee, and thou be found a liar."

The penalty for adding to Scripture is severe. Here in the book of Revelation, adding to this prophecy incurs bringing on yourself all of the plagues described under the seals, trumpets, and vials. God help those who do this and who are doing so right now.

The warning is clear! Everybody who is not rightly dividing the Word of Truth will be victims of their own false presumptions.

"And if any man shall take away from the words of the book of this prophecy, God shall take away his part from the tree of life, and out of the holy city, which are written in this book" (verse nineteen).

In like manner, if anyone is foolish enough to subtract anything from this book, that person (or persons) will not enter into the kingdom of God. Instead, they will be cast into the outer darkness, where they will suffer eternally.

"He who testifieth these things saith, Yea: I come quickly" (verse twenty).

Lastly, Jesus tells us that when He comes, He will come quickly and unannounced.

"Amen: come, Lord Jesus" (verse twenty, part b).

If we are truly led by the Holy Spirit, we should join in with John in the Bible's last prayer. Even so, come, Lord Jesus!

"The grace of the Lord Jesus be with the saints. Amen" (verse twenty-one).

It is fitting that John concludes the book of Revelation with this benediction. Endurance until the end will only be possible by the supply of grace from our Lord and Savior, Jesus Christ. This is the grace that every believer must draw on in hope for the return of Jesus Christ.

Amen so be it!

Afterword

Ann was adamant about having this book published as a witness to her husband Carleton's love of God and His Word. He prepared himself as a Christian who loved God and was willing to sacrifice whatever it took to be a man of God who rightly divided His Word and shared with as many as would listen.

About the Cover

John was banished to Patmos (an island southwest of Greece) from Ephesus by the Roman government for testifying about our Lord, Jesus Christ, and His resurrection. The island was mined and quarried by the slaves of the Roman government. The caverns on the island served as a shelter for the slaves.

Caran painted the cover to illustrate the light of Christ breaking through the darkened sky, conveying that Jesus is *the light of the world*. She imagined the island of Patmos as a bleak place of exile and hopelessness, without beauty. John is seated on a rock, writing what Jesus has instructed him to, as the soft waves of the Aegean Sea lap on the rocks and sandy shore.

Caran also illustrated the book with line drawings. A careful study was done to be as accurate as possible. She found it to be a great honor to contribute to her dad's book.

For the Glory of God

Thank you so very much for reading my husband's book! The message the book brings is one of hope, hope for your future and mine and those we love. While there is evil and darkness in the book of Revelation, there is much hope and many glorious promises.

It occurred to me that you, just like so many others, including Carleton and me at one time, thought you were a Christian. After all, we live in a Christian country, we go to church (sometimes), we put money in the offering plate, and do many other things that we consider will give us the title "Christian."

If you are not sure of your relationship with God and want to know how to be sure, here are some excellent scriptural verses from the book of Romans to lead you in the right direction:

"For all have sinned, and fall short of the glory of God" (Romans 3:23).

We all need salvation.

"But God commendeth his own love toward us, in that, while we were yet sinners, Christ died for us" (Romans 5:8).

Jesus loved us so much He died on the cross so that we would be saved.

"For the wages of sin is death; but the free gift of God is eternal life in Christ Jesus our Lord" (Romans 6:23).

A new life with Jesus is a gift; all we have to do is ask for it and accept the gift.

"But if it is by grace, it is no more of works: otherwise, grace is no more grace" (Romans 11:6).

God uses His grace to freely give us the gift of salvation through the sacrifice of His Son, Jesus, on the cross.

"But to him that worketh not, but believeth on him that justifieth the ungodly, his faith is reckoned for righteousness" (Romans 4:5).

Biography of Carleton Fletcher Burrows, Jr.

Carleton F. Burrows Jr. was born on a very bitter-cold winter day, February 5, 1934. He was born into a loving family: his mom, Mary, his eldest sisters, Doris and Ruth, and his youngest sister, Alice. The day that he was born, it was so cold in the house that Doctor Murphy didn't take his coat off until it was absolutely necessary. At times, with his coat on, he would get close to the small wood stove in the kitchen to get warm. When his front was warm, he would turn around to warm his back. Needless to say, there came a time when the aroma of burning wool began to fill the air. Doctor Murphy burned a hole in the back of his coat.

Carleton attended a one-room school not too far from home on Travilah Road, Rockville, Maryland. During his elementary years, he did so well that his teacher graduated him early to the next higher grade. The first time Carleton advanced, he handled it well; the second time, not so much—he became arrogant and cocky. His caring teacher decided that he needed to learn an important life lesson, and she took that second year away from him. He graduated from Richard Montgomery High School, Rockville, at age seventeen, with four years of perfect attendance and a straight grade A level status.

During those four years of high school, he was fortunate to take a course provided by, at that time, the Army Map Service of the federal government. He would have a job with them if he succeeded in his coursework. He was employed there for thirty-seven years. He had become a gifted cartographer. He served two years in the US Army. While at the Map Service, he was blessed to be chosen to map the back side of the moon. He and two other cartographers were asked to go to Houston, Texas, to do the charting for Apollo Eight.

Carleton and I were married in 1956. The Burrows family grew over the next six years; our daughter, Caran, and our son Carleton the third, "Butch," was born.

Caran loved fishing with her dad and watching him do wood and leatherwork. She had a great appreciation of his many artistic abilities. She enjoyed going along with the family during Civil War reenactments as a child. She was enthralled with and proud of her dad's involvement with the Apollo Lunar maps that he made. She loved camping with the family. Jumping waves at the beach with her dad was most memorable and fun. She viewed her dad as brilliant, funny, warm, loving, and caring. She thinks he was excellent at conveying ancient culture, history, and the original language of Scriptures with his teachings, which "painted" vivid scenes of biblical scriptures.

Butch adored his dad, and when he was three years old, he would get up every morning at six a.m. to hug his dad goodbye as he left for work. He would go back to bed and sleep.

Butch's favorite times with his dad were the many fishing and canoeing trips they took together on beautiful lakes and streams that were close by and in Canada.

One Saturday night, March 29, 1974, at a Teen Challenge rally, at age forty, Carleton gave his life to our Savior and Lord, Jesus Christ. He was forever changed. His appetite for a closer and closer and closer relationship with God was insatiable. When he was forty-two, God called him into the ministry. He studied at Washington Bible College in Lanham, Maryland, while working full time in Washington, DC. He loved to tell people that he, like Moses, wandered for forty years in the wilderness. Carleton went on to become a pastor, a mentor, and a Bible study leader. When choosing Bible studies, people almost always chose the book of Revelation.

On October 13, 2009, at 4:51 p.m., Carleton went home to be with his beloved Lord and Savior.

Notes

1. Flavius Josephus, *The Antiquities of the Jews* (1544).

2. William Barclay, *Letters to the Seven Churches* (Louisville, Kentucky: Westminster John Knox Press, 2001, 18.

3. Frederick A. Tatford, *The Patmos Letters* (Prophetic Witness Publishing House, 1969), 90.

4. *Encyclopaedia Britannica Online*, s.v. "Apollo," accessed February 12, 2022, https://www.britannica.com/topic/Apollo-Greek-mythology.

5. Alexander Hislop, *The Two Babylons* (Presbyterian Free Church of Scotland: 1853).

Study Notes

CPSIA information can be obtained
at www.ICGtesting.com
Printed in the USA
LVHW081918120522
718422LV00014B/394